Birnbaum's 95
Bermuda

A BIRNBAUM TRAVEL GUIDE

Alexandra Mayes Birnbaum
EDITORIAL CONSULTANT

Lois Spritzer
Editorial Director

Laura L. Brengelman
Managing Editor

Mary Callahan
Senior Editor

David Appell
Patricia Canole
Gene Gold
Jill Kadetsky
Susan McClung
Associate Editors

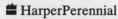 **HarperPerennial**
A Division of HarperCollinsPublishers

For Louis Birnbaum, who made the introductions.

BIRNBAUM'S BERMUDA 95. Copyright © 1994 by HarperCollins Publishers. All rights reserved. Printed in the United States of America. No part of this book may be used or reproduced in any manner whatsoever without written permission except in the case of brief quotations embodied in critical articles and reviews. For information address HarperCollins*Publishers*, 10 East 53rd Street, New York, NY 10022.

FIRST EDITION

ISSN 0749-2561 (Birnbaum Travel Guides)
ISSN 1055-5684 (Bermuda)
ISBN 0-06-278168-5 (pbk.)

94 95 96 97 ❖/CW 5 4 3 2 1

Cover design © Drenttel Doyle Partners
Cover photograph © George Hunter/Allstock

BIRNBAUM TRAVEL GUIDES

Bahamas, and Turks & Caicos
Berlin
Bermuda
Boston
Canada
Cancun, Cozumel & Isla Mujeres
Caribbean
Chicago
Disneyland
Eastern Europe
Europe
Europe for Business Travelers
France
Germany
Great Britain
Hawaii
Ireland
Italy
London
Los Angeles
Mexico
Miami & Ft. Lauderdale
Montreal & Quebec City
New Orleans
New York
Paris
Portugal
Rome
San Francisco
Santa Fe & Taos
South America
Spain
United States
USA for Business Travelers
Walt Disney World
Walt Disney World for Kids, By Kids
Washington, DC

Contributing Editors

David Allen
Judith Wadson
Laurie Werner

Maps

B. Andrew Mudryk

Contents

Diversions

*A selective guide to a variety of unexpected
pleasures, pinpointing the best places to pursue them.*

Exceptional Pleasures and Treasures

Directions

*The most delightful walks through Bermuda's
most scenic parishes—all nine of them.*

Foreword

Long before "quality time" became popular buzz words among brooding analysts, overworked parents, and lonely children, my husband, Steve Birnbaum, was taken to Bermuda. He was 8 years old. My first Bermuda foray was on my own at the age of 21, but for each of us, a love affair with Bermuda began the minute we arrived. Nothing can dampen my enthusiasm for returning to Bermuda anytime I can fabricate an excuse to do so.

Oh, Bermuda has changed, but so compelling are its unique lures that even the largest and least appropriate hotel developments can be tolerated for the simple reason that they happily cocxist with oleander and hibiscus. Bermuda remains the most sophisticated of vacation islands, where Bermudians make visitors feel welcome in ways that no other island even approaches. And I know that at least part of the enthusiasm of this welcome is spawned by self-interest; there's not a single soul on the island of Bermuda whose livelihood and well-being do not depend in some measure on the maintenance of tourist affection for the island. But even if the hospitality of Bermudians were entirely contrived, visitors would have to admit that the local population comprised the greatest company of accomplished actors the world had ever seen!

Bermuda's very proximity to the US mainland only exaggerates the island's appeal. Barely a 90-minute flight from anywhere along the eastern US coastline, it is the perfect escape from today's pressured lifestyles. Here is the best place I know for a long weekend in a "foreign" environment, the sort of brief holiday that tends to recharge internal batteries and restores both soul and spirit. Clearly, Bermuda is a favorite destination of mine, and it has been our aim to produce a guide that accurately and insightfully projects the appeals and allures of this unique holiday place—as well as documenting its occasional blemishes.

That's why we've tried to create a guide that's specifically organized, written, and edited for today's demanding modern traveler, one for whom qualitative information is infinitely more desirable than mere quantities of unappraised data. We realize that it's impossible for any single travel writer to visit thousands of restaurants (and nearly as many hotels) in any given year and provide accurate appraisals of each. And even if it were physically possible for one human being to survive such an itinerary, it would of necessity have to be done at a dead sprint, and the perceptions derived therefrom would probably be less valid than those of any other intelligent individual visiting the same establishments. It is, therefore, both impractical and undesirable (especially in a large, annually revised and updated guidebook *series* such as we offer) to have only one person provide all the data on the entire world. Instead, we have chosen what we like to describe as the "thee and me" approach to restaurant and hotel evaluation and, to a somewhat more limited degree, to the sites and sights we have included our text. What this really reflects is personal sampling tempered by intelligent counsel from informed local sources.

This guidebook is directed to the "visitor," and such elements as restaurants have been specifically picked to provide the visitor with a representative, enlightening, and above all pleasant experience. Since so many extraneous considerations can affect the reception and service accorded a regular restaurant patron, our choices can in no way be construed as an exhaustive guide to resident dining. We think we've listed all the best places, in various price ranges, but they were chosen with a visitor's enjoyment in mind.

Other evidence of how we've tried to tailor our text to reflect modern travel habits is apparent in the section we call DIVERSIONS. Where once it was common for travelers to spend an island visit nailed to a single spot, today's traveler is more likely to want to pursue a special interest or to venture off the beaten track. In response to this trend, we have collected a series of exceptional experiences so that it is no longer necessary to wade through a pound or two of superfluous prose just to find unexpected pleasures and treasures.

Finally, I also should point out that every good travel guide is a living enterprise; that is, no part of this text is carved in stone. In our annual revisions, we refine, expand, and further hone all our material to serve your travel needs better. To this end, no contribution is of greater value to us than your personal reaction to what we have written, as well as information reflecting your own experiences while using the book. Please write to us at 10 E. 53rd St., New York, NY 10022.

We sincerely hope to hear from you.

Alexandra Mayes Birnbaum

ALEXANDRA MAYES BIRNBAUM, editorial consultant to the *Birnbaum Travel Guides,* worked with her late husband Stephen Birnbaum as co-editor of the series. She has been a world traveler since childhood and is known for her travel reports on radio on what's hot and what's not.

Bermuda

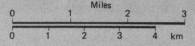

BERMUDA

Miles

0   1   2   3

0   1   2   3   4   km

~   Selected beaches
◼   Selected resorts, hotels, etc.
✳   Golf courses
◻   Other points of interest

A T L A N T I C

IRELAND
ISLAND
NORTH   ◻ H.M. Dockyard

              Grassy Bay

              IRELAND
Black Bay   ISLAND
              SOUTH

                                      Clarence
                                      Cove
Somerset   Mangrove   Boaz   Government ◻
Long Bay   Bay   Island   Spanish Point   House   Ft.
         ◻ Somerset   Green Bay   PEMBROKE ◻ Hamilton
           Village   ◻
         Library   SANDYS   Hamilton
Margaret's   Princess
Bay   (SOMERSET)   Agar's I.   Hamilton Harbour
         SOMERSET   G R E A T   Triming
         ISLAND   Long I.   Hill
      Ft.   Hawkins I.   Hinson Salt ◼ Newstead
      ◻ Scaur   S O U N D   Nelly I. I. Kettle
    Eby's ◻ Cathedral Rocks   Ports Marshall Bay   PAGET
         ◼ Lantana   Burt I. I. I.   ◼ Fourways Elbow
         Colony   Darrell's   Beach
         Somerset Bridge   Grace I.   I.   ◼ Belmont Horizons ◼
                  Naval Air   ✳   Coral
                  Station Annex   WARWICK   Beach Club
                                                   ◼   Surfside Beach
              George's   ✳ Riddell's   Marley
              Bay   Bay G.C.   Beach
Pompano   ✳ Port Royal LITTLE SOUND   ~ Marley Beach
Beach   G.C.   Riddell's
West   Bay   ~ Mermaid Beach
Whale Bay   Frank's   Black   ✳   ~ Warwick Long Bay
              Bay   Bay   Southampton ~ Chaplin Bay
                    Gibb's Hill ◻ Princess Stonehole Bay
         SOUTHAMPTON Lighthouse   ~ Horseshoe Bay
                    Reefs   ~ East Whale Bay
         Church Christian Sonesta
         Bay   Bay   Beach

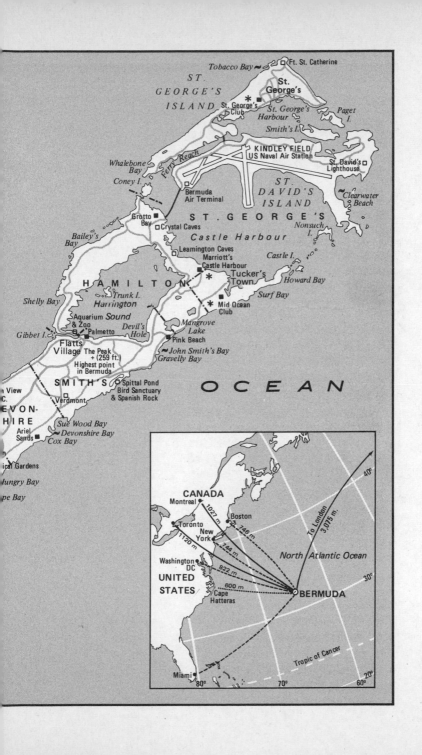

Tobacco Bay 〰 □ Ft. St. Catherine

ST. GEORGE'S ISLAND

St.
George's

✳ St. George's
□ Club

*St. George's
Harbour*

*Paget
I.*

Smith's I.

KINDLEY FIELD
US Naval Air Station

St. David's
□ Lighthouse

*Whalebone
Bay*

Ferry Reach

Coney I.

□ Bermuda
Air Terminal

*ST.
DAVID'S
ISLAND*

*Clearwater
Beach*

Grotto
Bay □
□ Crystal Caves

ST. GEORGE'S

Castle Harbour

*Nonsuch
I.*

*Bailey's
Bay*

□ Leamington Caves
Marriott's
■ Castle Harbour
✳

Castle I.

H A M I L T O N
*Tucker's
Town*

Howard Bay

■

Shelly Bay

△ *Trunk I.*
Harrington

Surf Bay

Aquarium *Sound*
& Zoo □
□ ■ Palmetto

*Devil's
Hole*

✳ ■ Mid Ocean
Club

Gibbet I. ○

*Mangrove
Lake*

**Flatts
Village** The Peak
+ (259 ft.)
Highest point
in Bermuda

● Pink Beach

〰 *John Smith's Bay*
Gravelly Bay

O C E A N

View
C.

SMITH'S

○ Spittal Pond
Bird Sanctuary
& Spanish Rock

DEVON-
HIRE

□ Verdmont

Sue Wood Bay
〰 *Devonshire Bay*
Cox Bay

*Ariel
Sands* ■

ical Gardens

ungry Bay

pe Bay

CANADA
Montreal ●

1027 m

Boston
●

746 m

**UNITED
STATES**

Toronto ●
New
York ●

744 m

1120 m

North Atlantic Ocean

Washington ●
DC

822 m

BERMUDA

600 m

Cape
Hatteras

To London
3,075 m.

40°

30°

Miami ●

Tropic of Cancer

20°

80°

70°

60°

How to Use This Guide

A great deal of care has gone into the special organization of this guide-book, and we believe it represents a real breakthrough in the presentation of travel material.

Our text is divided into four basic sections, in order to present information in the best way on every possible aspect of a Bermuda vacation. Our aim is to highlight what's where and to provide basic information—how, when, where, how much, and what's best—to assist you in making the most intelligent choices possible.

Here is a brief summary of what you can expect to find in each section. We believe that you will find both your travel planning and on-island enjoyment enhanced by having this book at your side.

GETTING READY TO GO

A mini-encyclopedia of practical travel facts with all the precise data necessary to create a successful Bermuda holiday. Here you will find how to get where you're going, currency information and exchange rates, plus selected resources—including useful publications, and companies and organizations specializing in discount and special-interest travel—providing a wealth of information and assistance useful both before and during your trip.

THE ISLAND

Our individual report on Bermuda offers a short-stay guide, including an essay introducing the island as a contemporary place to visit; *Bermuda At-a-Glance* contains a site-by-site survey of the most important, interesting, and sometimes most eclectic sights to see and things to do; *Local Sources and Resources* is a concise listing of pertinent tourist information, such as the address of the local tourist office, which sightseeing tours to take, where to find the best nightspot, to play golf, to rent scuba equipment, to find the best beach, or to get a taxi. *Best on the Island* lists our collection of cost-and-quality choices of the best places to eat and sleep on a variety of budgets.

DIVERSIONS

This section is designed to help travelers find the best places to engage in a variety of exceptional experiences for the mind and body, without having to wade through endless pages of unrelated text. In every case, our particular suggestions are intended to guide you to that special place where the quality of experience is likely to be highest.

DIRECTIONS

Here are 9 walking or biking itineraries that follow the most evocative routes and roads, past the most spectacular natural wonders, covering the most historic parishes in Bermuda. DIRECTIONS is the only section of this book that is organized geographically; itineraries can be connected for longer trips or used individually for short, intensive explorations.

To use this book to full advantage, take a few minutes to read the table of contents and random entries in each section to get a firsthand feel for how it all fits together. You will find that the sections of this book are building blocks designed to help you put together the best possible trip. Use them selectively as a tool, a source of ideas, a reference work for accurate facts, and a guidebook to the best buys, the most exciting sights, the most pleasant accommodations, the tastiest foods—*the best travel experience* that you can possibly have.

Getting Ready to Go

Getting Ready to Go

When to Go

Bermuda has a moderate year-round climate. Although the weather is best during the peak travel season (April through October), even the cooler winter months can be pleasant. Hurricanes may occur any time between June and November, but are most common in September. Travel during the off-season and shoulder seasons (the months immediately before and after the peak months) offers relatively fair weather and smaller crowds, and often is less expensive.

If you have a touch-tone phone, you can call *The Weather Channel Connection* (phone: 900-WEATHER) for current worldwide weather forecasts. This service, available from *The Weather Channel* (2600 Cumberland Pkwy., Atlanta, GA 30339; phone: 404-434-6800), costs 95¢ per minute; the charge will appear on your phone bill.

Traveling by Plane

SCHEDULED FLIGHTS

Leading airlines offering flights between the US and Bermuda include *American, Continental, Delta, Northwest, United,* and *USAir.*

FARES The great variety of airfares can be reduced to the following basic categories: first class, business class (not usually available on flights to Bermuda), coach (also called economy or tourist class), excursion or discount, and standby, as well as various promotional fares. For information on applicable fares and restrictions, contact the airlines listed above or ask your travel agent. Most airfares are offered for a limited time; once you've found the lowest fare for which you can qualify, purchase your ticket as soon as possible.

RESERVATIONS Reconfirmation is strongly recommended for all international flights. It is essential that you confirm your round-trip reservations—*especially the return leg.*

SEATING Airline seats usually are assigned on a first-come, first-served basis at check-in, although you may be able to reserve a seat when purchasing your ticket. Seating charts sometimes are available from airlines and also are included in the *Airline Seating Guide* (Carlson Publishing Co., 11132 Los Alamitos Blvd., Los Alamitos, CA 90720; phone: 310-493-4877).

SMOKING US law prohibits smoking on flights scheduled for six hours or less within the US and its territories on both domestic and international carriers. These restrictions do not apply to nonstop flights between the US and international destinations, although a number of US carriers have independently banned smoking on some flights. For example, at press time, *Continental, Delta, Northwest,* and *USAir* prohibited smoking on all flights to Bermuda. A free wallet-size guide that describes the rights of nonsmokers under current regulations is available from *ASH (Action on Smoking and Health;* DOT Card, 2013 H St. NW, Washington, DC 20006; phone: 202-659-4310).

SPECIAL MEALS When making your reservation, you can request one of the airline's alternate menu choices for no additional charge. Though not always required, it's a good idea to reconfirm your request the day before departure.

BAGGAGE On major international carriers, passengers usually are allowed to carry on board one bag that will fit under a seat or in an overhead bin and to check two bags in the cargo hold. Specific regulations regarding dimensions and weight restrictions vary among airlines, but a checked bag usually cannot exceed 62 inches in combined dimensions (length, width, and depth) or weigh more than 70 pounds. There may be charges for additional, oversize, or overweight luggage, and for special equipment or sporting gear. Note that baggage allowances may be more limited for children (depending on the percentage of full adult fare paid). Check that the tags the airline attaches are correctly coded for your destination.

CHARTER FLIGHTS

By booking blocks of seats on specially arranged flights, charter operators frequently offer travelers bargain airfares. If you do fly on a charter, however, read the contract's fine print carefully. Federal regulations permit charter operators to cancel a flight or to assess surcharges of as much as 10% of the airfare up to 10 days before departure. You usually must book in advance, and once set, no changes in flight plans are permitted, so invest in trip cancellation insurance. Also, make your check out to the company's escrow account, which provides some protection for your funds in the event that the charter operator fails. For further information, consult the publication *Jax Fax* (397 Post Rd., Darien, CT 06820; phone: 203-655-8746; fax: 203-655-6257).

DISCOUNTS ON SCHEDULED FLIGHTS

COURIER TRAVEL In return for arranging to accompany some kind of freight, a traveler pays only a portion of the total airfare (and sometimes a small registration fee). One agency that matches up would-be couriers with courier companies is *Now Voyager* (74 Varick St., Suite 307, New York, NY 10013; phone: 212-431-1616; fax: 212-334-5243).

Courier Companies

Discount Travel International (169 W. 81st St., New York, NY 10024; phone: 212-362-3636; fax: 212-362-3236; and 801 Alton Rd., Suite 1, Miami Beach, FL 33139; phone: 305-538-1616; fax: 305-673-9376).

F.B. On Board Courier Club (10225 Ryan Ave., Suite 103, Dorval, Quebec H9P 1A2, Canada; phone: 514-633-0740; fax: 514-633-0735).

Halbart Express (147-05 176th St., Jamaica, NY 11434; phone: 718-656-8279; fax: 718-244-0559).

Midnite Express (925 W. Hyde Park Blvd., Inglewood, CA 90302; phone: 310-672-1100; fax: 310-671-0107).

Way to Go Travel (6679 Sunset Blvd., Hollywood, CA 90028; phone: 213-466-1126; fax: 213-466-8994).

Publications

Insiders Guide to Air Courier Bargains, by Kelly Monaghan (The Intrepid Traveler, PO Box 438, New York, NY 10034; phone: 800-356-9315 for orders only; 212-569-1081 for information; fax: 212-942-6687).

Travel Unlimited (PO Box 1058, Allston, MA 02134-1058; no phone).

CONSOLIDATORS AND BUCKET SHOPS These companies buy blocks of tickets from airlines and sell them at a discount to travel agents or directly to consumers. Since many bucket shops operate on a thin margin, be sure to check a company's record with the *Better Business Bureau*—before parting with any money.

Council Charter (205 E. 42nd St., New York, NY 10017; phone: 800-800-8222 or 212-661-0311; fax: 212-972-0194).

International Adventures (60 E. 42nd St., Room 763, New York, NY 10165; phone: 212-599-0577; fax: 212-599-3288).

Travac Tours and Charters (989 Ave. of the Americas, New York, NY 10018; phone: 800-872-8800 or 212-563-3303; fax: 212-563-3631).

Unitravel (1177 N. Warson Rd., St. Louis, MO 63132; phone: 800-325-2222 or 314-569-0900; fax: 314-569-2503).

LAST-MINUTE TRAVEL CLUBS Members of such clubs receive information on imminent trips and other bargain travel opportunities. There usually is an annual fee, although a few clubs offer free membership. Despite the names of some of the clubs listed below, you don't have to wait until literally the last minute to make travel plans.

Discount Travel International (114 Forrest Ave., Suite 203, Narberth, PA 19072; phone: 215-668-7184; fax: 215-668-9182).

Last Minute Travel (1249 Boylston St., Boston, MA 02215; phone: 800-LAST-MIN or 617-267-9800; fax: 617-424-1943).

Moment's Notice (425 Madison Ave., New York, NY 10017; phone: 212-486-0500/1/2/3; fax: 212-486-0783).

Spur of the Moment Cruises (411 N. Harbor Blvd., Suite 302, San Pedro, CA 90731; phone: 800-4-CRUISES or 310-521-1070 in California; 800-343-1991 elsewhere in the US; 24-hour hotline: 310-521-1060; fax: 310-521-1061).

Traveler's Advantage (3033 S. Parker Rd., Suite 900, Aurora, CO 80014; phone: 800-548-1116 or 800-835-8747; fax: 303-368-3985).

Vacations to Go (1502 Augusta Dr., Suite 415, Houston, TX 77057; phone: 713-974-2121 in Texas; 800-338-4962 elsewhere in the US; fax: 713-974-0445).

Worldwide Discount Travel Club (1674 Meridian Ave., Miami Beach, FL 33139; phone: 305-534-2082; fax: 305-534-2070).

GENERIC AIR TRAVEL These organizations operate much like an ordinary airline standby service, except that they offer seats on not one but several scheduled and charter airlines. One pioneer of generic flights is *Airhitch* (2790 Broadway, Suite 100, New York, NY 10025; phone: 212-864-2000).

BARTERED TRAVEL SOURCES Barter—the exchange of commodities or services in lieu of cash payment—is a common practice among travel suppliers. Companies that have obtained travel services through barter may sell these services at substantial discounts to travel clubs, who pass along the savings to members. One organization offering bartered travel opportunities is *Travel World Leisure Club* (225 W. 34th St., Suite 909, New York, NY 10122; phone: 800-444-TWLC or 212-239-4855; fax: 212-564-5158).

CONSUMER PROTECTION

Passengers whose complaints have not been satisfactorily addressed by the airline can contact the *US Department of Transportation* (*DOT;* Consumer Affairs Division, 400 Seventh St. SW, Room 10405, Washington, DC 20590; phone: 202-366-2220). Also see *Fly Rights* (Publication #050-000-00513-5; *US Government Printing Office,* PO Box 371954, Pittsburgh, PA 15250-7954; phone: 202-783-3238; fax: 202-512-2250). If you have safety-related questions or concerns, write to the *Federal Aviation Administration* (*FAA;* 800 Independence Ave. SW, Washington, DC, 20591) or call the *FAA Consumer Hotline* (phone: 800-322-7873). If you have a complaint against a local travel service in Bermuda, contact the *Bermuda Department of Tourism* (Global House, 43 Church St., Hamilton HM-12, Bermuda; phone: 809-292-0023; fax: 809-292-7537).

Traveling by Ship

Your cruise fare usually includes all meals, recreational activities, and entertainment. Shore excursions are available at extra cost, and can be booked in advance or once you're on board. An important factor in the price of a cruise is the location (and sometimes the size) of your cabin. Charts issued by the *Cruise Lines International Association* (*CLIA;* 500 Fifth Ave., Suite

1407, New York, NY 10110; phone: 212-921-0066; fax: 212-921-0549) provide information on ship layouts and facilities and are available at some *CLIA*-affiliated travel agencies.

The *US Public Health Service (PHS)* inspects all passenger vessels calling at US ports; for the most recent summary or a particular inspection report, write to Chief, Vessel Sanitation Program, National Center for Environmental Health (1015 N. America Way, Room 107, Miami, FL 33132; phone: 305-536-4307). Most cruise ships have a doctor on board, plus medical facilities.

For further information on cruises and cruise lines, consult *Ocean and Cruise News* (PO Box 92, Stamford, CT 06904; phone and fax: 203-329-2787). And for a free listing of travel agencies specializing in cruises, contact the *National Association of Cruise Only Agencies* (*NACOA;* 3191 Coral Way, Suite 630, Miami, FL 33145; phone: 305-446-7732; fax: 305-446-9732).

International Cruise Lines

Chandris Celebrity and Chandris Fantasy Cruises (5200 Blue Lagoon Dr., Miami, FL 33126; phone: 800-437-3111 or 305-262-6677; fax: 305-262-2677).

Crystal Cruises (2121 Ave. of the Stars, Los Angeles, CA 90067; phone: 800-446-6645 or 310-785-9300; fax: 310-785-0011).

Cunard (555 Fifth Ave., New York, NY 10017; phone: 800-5-CUNARD or 800-221-4770; fax: 718-786-0038).

Dolphin Royal Majesty Cruise Line (901 S. America Way, Miami, FL 33132; phone: 800-222-1003; fax: 305-358-4807).

Norwegian Cruise Line (95 Merrick Way, Coral Gables, FL 33134; phone: 800-327-7030; fax: 305-443-2464).

Regency Cruises (260 Madison Ave., New York, NY 10016; phone: 212-972-4774 in New York State; 800-388-5500 elsewhere in the US; fax: 800-388-8833).

Royal Caribbean Cruise Lines (1050 Caribbean Way, Miami, FL 33132; phone: 800-432-6559 in Florida; 800-327-6700 elsewhere in the US; fax: 800-722-5680).

Package Tours

A package is a collection of travel services that can be purchased in a single transaction. Its principal advantages are convenience and economy— the cost usually is lower than that of the same services purchased separately. Tour programs generally can be divided into two categories: escorted or locally hosted (with a set itinerary) and independent (usually more flexible).

When considering a package tour, read the brochure *carefully* to determine exactly what is included and any conditions that may apply, and check the company's record with the *Better Business Bureau.* The *United States Tour Operators Association (USTOA;* 211 E. 51st St., Suite 12B, New York, NY 10022; phone: 212-750-7371; fax: 212-421-1285) also can be helpful in determining a package tour operator's reliability. As with charter flights, to safeguard your funds, always make your check out to the company's escrow account.

Many tour operators offer packages focused on special interests such as the arts, nature study, sports, and other recreations. *All Adventure Travel* (5589 Arapahoe St., Suite 208, Boulder, CO 80303; phone: 800-537-4025 or 303-440-7924; fax: 303-440-4160) represents such specialized packagers; some also are listed in the *Specialty Travel Index* (305 San Anselmo Ave., Suite 313, San Anselmo, CA 94960; phone: 415-459-4900 in California; 800-442-4922 elsewhere in the US; fax: 415-459-4974). A variety of package tours to Bermuda also are listed in the *Island Vacation Catalog,* issued by *TourScan* (PO Box 2367, Darien, CT 06820; phone: 800-962-2080 or 203-655-8091; fax: 203-655-6689).

Package Tour Operators

Adventure Tours (9818-B Liberty Rd., Randallstown, MD 21133; phone: 410-922-7000 in Baltimore; 800-638-9040 elsewhere in the US; fax: 410-521-6968).

American Airlines FlyAAway Vacations (4200 Amon Carter Blvd., PO Box 2215, Ft. Worth, TX 76155; phone: 800-321-2121).

Apple Vacations East (7 Campus Blvd., PO Box 6500, Newtown Sq., PA 19073; phone: 800-727-3400; fax: 215-359-6524).

Certified Vacations (110 E. Broward Blvd., Ft. Lauderdale, FL 33302; phone: 800-233-7260 or 305-522-1440; fax: 305-357-4687).

Continental Grand Destinations (465 Smith St., Farmingdale, NY 11735; phone: 800-634-5555).

GoGo Tours (69 Spring St., Ramsey, NJ 07446-0507; phone: 201-934-3500; fax: 201-934-3764).

Liberty Travel (check the yellow pages or contact the central office for the nearest location: 69 Spring St., Ramsey, NJ 07446; phone: 201-934-3500; fax: 201-934-3888).

Travel Impressions (465 Smith St., Farmingdale, NY 11735; phone: 800-284-0044).

Worldwide Nordic (PO Box 1129, Maplewood, NJ 07040; phone: 201-378-9170; fax: 201-378-9193).

Insurance

The first person with whom you should discuss travel insurance is your own insurance broker. You may discover that the insurance you already carry protects you adequately while traveling and that you need little additional coverage. If you charge travel services, the credit card company also may provide some insurance coverage (and other safeguards).

Types of Travel Insurance

Baggage and personal effects insurance: Protects your bags and their contents in case of damage or theft at any point during your travels.

Personal accident and sickness insurance: Covers cases of illness, injury, or death in an accident while traveling.

Trip cancellation and interruption insurance: Guarantees a refund if you must cancel a trip; may reimburse you for additional travel costs incurred in catching up with a tour or traveling home early.

Default and/or bankruptcy insurance: Provides coverage in the event of default and/or bankruptcy on the part of the tour operator, airline, or other travel supplier.

Flight insurance: Covers accidental injury or death while flying.

Automobile insurance: Provides collision, theft, property damage, and personal liability protection while driving.

Combination policies: Include any or all of the above.

Disabled Travelers

Make travel arrangements well in advance. Specify to all services involved the nature of your disability to determine if there are accommodations and facilities that meet your needs.

Organizations

ACCENT on Living (PO Box 700, Bloomington, IL 61702; phone: 800-787-8444 or 309-378-2961; fax: 309-378-4420).

Access: The Foundation for Accessibility by the Disabled (PO Box 356, Malverne, NY 11565; phone and fax: 516-887-5798).

American Foundation for the Blind (15 W. 16th St., New York, NY 10011; phone: 800-232-5463 or 212-620-2147; fax: 212-727-7418).

Information Center for Individuals with Disabilities (Ft. Point Pl., 27-43 Wormwood St., Boston, MA 02210; phone: 800-462-5015 in Massachusetts; 617-727-5540 elsewhere in the US; TDD: 617-345-9743; fax: 617-345-5318).

Mobility International USA (*MIUSA;* PO Box 3551, Eugene, OR 97403; phone and TDD: 503-343-1284; fax: 503-343-6812; main office: 228 Borough High St., London SE1 1JX, England; phone: 44-71-403-5688; fax: 44-71-378-1292).

Moss Rehabilitation Hospital Travel Information Service (*telephone referrals only;* phone: 215-456-9600; TDD: 215-456-9602).

National Rehabilitation Information Center (8455 Colesville Rd., Suite 935, Silver Spring, MD 20910; phone: 301-588-9284; fax: 301-587-1967).

Paralyzed Veterans of America (PVA; PVA/ATTS Program, 801 18th St. NW, Washington, DC 20006; phone: 202-872-1300 in Washington, DC; 800-424-8200 elsewhere in the US; fax: 202-785-4452).

Royal Association for Disability and Rehabilitation (RADAR; 12 City Forum, 250 City Rd., London EC1 V8AF, England; phone: 44-71-250-3222).

Society for the Advancement of Travel for the Handicapped (SATH; 347 Fifth Ave., Suite 610, New York, NY 10016; phone: 212-447-7284; fax: 212-725-8253).

Travel Industry and Disabled Exchange (TIDE; 5435 Donna Ave., Tarzana, CA 91356; phone: 818-368-5648).

Publications

Access Travel: A Guide to the Accessibility of Airport Terminals (Consumer Information Center, Dept. 578Z, Pueblo, CO 81009; phone: 719-948-3334).

Air Transportation of Handicapped Persons (Publication #AC-120-32; *US Department of Transportation,* Distribution Unit, Publications Section, M-443-2, 400 Seventh St. SW, Washington, DC 20590; phone: 202-366-0039).

The Diabetic Traveler (PO Box 8223 RW, Stamford, CT 06905; phone: 203-327-5832; fax: 203-975-1748).

Directory of Travel Agencies for the Disabled and Travel for the Disabled, both by Helen Hecker (Twin Peaks Press, PO Box 129, Vancouver, WA 98666; phone: 800-637-CALM or 206-694-2462; fax: 206-696-3210).

Guide to Traveling with Arthritis (Upjohn Company, PO Box 989, Dearborn, MI 48121; phone: 800-253-9860).

Handicapped Travel Newsletter (PO Box 269, Athens, TX 75751; phone and fax: 903-677-1260).

Handi-Travel: A Resource Book for Disabled and Elderly Travellers, by Cinnie Noble (*Canadian Rehabilitation Council for the Disabled,* 45 Sheppard Ave. E., Suite 801, Toronto, Ontario M2N 5W9, Canada; phone and TDD: 416-250-7490; fax: 416-229-1371).

Incapacitated Passengers Air Travel Guide (*International Air Transport Association,* Publications Sales Department, 2000 Peel St., Montreal, Quebec H3A 2R4, Canada; phone: 514-844-6311; fax: 514-844-5286).

Ticket to Safe Travel (*American Diabetes Association,* 1660 Duke St., Alexandria, VA 22314; phone: 800-232-3472 or 703-549-1500; fax: 703-836-7439).

Travel for the Patient with Chronic Obstructive Pulmonary Disease (Dr. Harold Silver, 1601 18th St. NW, Washington, DC 20009; phone: 202-667-0134; fax: 202-667-0148).

Travel Tips for Hearing-Impaired People (*American Academy of Otolaryngology,* 1 Prince St., Alexandria, VA 22314; phone: 703-836-4444; fax: 703-683-5100).

Travel Tips for People with Arthritis (*Arthritis Foundation,* 1314 Spring St. NW, Atlanta, GA 30309; phone: 800-283-7800 or 404-872-7100; fax: 404-872-0457).

Traveling Like Everybody Else: A Practical Guide for Disabled Travelers, by Jacqueline Freedman and Susan Gersten (Modan Publishing, PO Box 1202, Bellmore, NY 11710; phone: 516-679-1380; fax: 516-679-1448).

Package Tour Operators

Accessible Journeys (35 W. Sellers Ave., Ridley Park, PA 19078; phone: 800-846-4537 or 215-521-0339; fax: 215-521-6959).

Accessible Tours/Directions Unlimited (Lois Bonnani, 720 N. Bedford Rd., Bedford Hills, NY 10507; phone: 800-533-5343 or 914-241-1700; fax: 914-241-0243).

Beehive Business and Leisure Travel (1130 W. Center St., N. Salt Lake, UT 84054; phone: 800-777-5727 or 801-292-4445; fax: 801-298-9460).

Classic Travel Service (8 W. 40th St., New York, NY 10018; phone: 212-869-2560 in New York State; 800-247-0909 elsewhere in the US; fax: 212-944-4493).

Dialysis at Sea Cruises (611 Barry Pl., Indian Rocks Beach, FL 34635; phone: 800-775-1333 or 813-596-4614; fax: 813-596-0203).

Evergreen Travel Service (4114 198th St. SW, Suite 13, Lynnwood, WA 98036-6742; phone: 800-435-2288 or 206-776-1184; fax: 206-775-0728).

Flying Wheels Travel (143 W. Bridge St., PO Box 382, Owatonna, MN 55060; phone: 800-535-6790 or 507-451-5005; fax: 507-451-1685).

Good Neighbor Travel Service (124 S. Main St., Viroqua, WI 54665; phone: 800-338-3245 or 608-637-2128; fax: 608-637-3030).

The Guided Tour (7900 Old York Rd., Suite 114B, Elkins Park, PA 19117-2339; phone: 800-783-5841 or 215-782-1370; fax: 215-635-2637).

Hinsdale Travel (201 E. Ogden Ave., Hinsdale, IL 60521; phone: 708-325-1335 or 708-469-7349; fax: 708-325-1342).

MedEscort International (*ABE International Airport,* PO Box 8766, Allentown, PA 18105-8766; phone: 800-255-7182 or 215-791-3111; fax: 215-791-9189).

Prestige World Travel (5710-X High Point Rd., Greensboro, NC 27407; phone: 800-476-7737 or 910-292-6690; fax: 910-632-9404).

Sprout (893 Amsterdam Ave., New York, NY 10025; phone: 212-222-9575; fax: 212-222-9768).

Weston Travel Agency (134 N. Cass Ave., PO Box 1050, Westmont, IL 60559; phone: 708-968-2513 in Illinois; 800-633-3725 elsewhere in the US; fax: 708-968-2539).

Single Travelers

The travel industry is not very fair to people who vacation by themselves—they often end up paying more than those traveling in pairs. There are services catering to single travelers, however, that match travel companions, offer travel arrangements with shared accommodations, and provide information and discounts. Useful publications include *Going Solo* (Doerfer Communications, PO Box 123, Apalachicola, FL 32329; phone and fax: 904-653-8848) and *Traveling on Your Own,* by Eleanor Berman (Random House, Order Dept., 400 Hahn Rd., Westminster, MD 21157; phone: 800-733-3000; fax: 800-659-2436).

Organizations and Companies

Gallivanting (515 E. 79th St., Suite 20F, New York, NY 10021; phone: 800-933-9699 or 212-988-0617; fax: 212-988-0144).

Globus and Cosmos (5301 S. Federal Circle, Littleton, CO 80123; phone: 800-221-0090 or 800-556-5454; fax: 800-289-4646).

Jane's International and Sophisticated Women Travelers (2603 Bath Ave., Brooklyn, NY 11214; phone: 718-266-2045; fax: 718-266-4062).

Marion Smith Singles (611 Prescott Pl., N. Woodmere, NY 11581; phone: 516-791-4852, 516-791-4865, or 212-944-2112; fax: 516-791-4879).

Partners-in-Travel (11660 Chenault St., Suite 119, Los Angeles, CA 90049; phone: 310-476-4869).

Singles in Motion (545 W. 236th St., Riverdale, NY 10463; phone and fax: 718-884-4464).

Singleworld (401 Theodore Fremd Ave., Rye, NY 10580; phone: 800-223-6490 or 914-967-3334; fax: 914-967-7395).

Solo Flights (63 High Noon Rd., Weston, CT 06883; phone: 800-266-1566 or 203-226-9993).

Suddenly Singles Tours (161 Dreiser Loop, Bronx, NY 10475; phone: 718-379-8800 in New York City; 800-859-8396 elsewhere in the US; fax: 718-379-8858).

Travel Companion Exchange (PO Box 833, Amityville, NY 11701; phone: 516-454-0880; fax: 516-454-0170).

Travel Companions (Atrium Financial Center, 1515 N. Federal Hwy., Suite 300, Boca Raton, FL 33432; phone: 800-383-7211 or 407-393-6448; fax: 407-451-8560).

Travel in Two's (239 N. Broadway, Suite 3, N. Tarrytown, NY 10591; phone: 914-631-8301 in New York State; 800-692-5252 elsewhere in the US).

Umbrella Singles (PO Box 157, Woodbourne, NY 12788; phone: 800-537-2797 or 914-434-6871; fax: 914-434-3532).

Older Travelers

GETTING READY TO GO

Special discounts and more free time are just two factors that have given older travelers a chance to see the world at affordable prices. Many travel suppliers offer senior discounts—sometimes only to members of certain senior citizens organizations (which provide benefits of their own). When considering a particular package, make sure the facilities—and the pace of the tour—match your needs and physical condition.

Publications

Going Abroad: 101 Tips for Mature Travelers (*Grand Circle Travel,* 347 Congress St., Boston, MA 02210; phone: 800-221-2610 or 617-350-7500; fax: 617-423-0445).

The Mature Traveler (PO Box 50820, Reno, NV 89513-0820; phone: 702-786-7419).

Take a Camel to Lunch and Other Adventures for Mature Travelers, by Nancy O'Connell (Bristol Publishing Enterprises, PO Box 1737, San Leandro, CA 94577; phone: 510-895-4461 in California; 800-346-4889 elsewhere in the US; fax: 510-895-4459).

Unbelievably Good Deals & Great Adventures That You Absolutely Can't Get Unless You're Over 50, by Joan Rattner Heilman (Contemporary Books, 1200 Stetson Ave., Chicago, IL 60601; phone: 312-782-9181; fax: 312-540-4687).

Organizations

American Association of Retired Persons (*AARP;* 601 E St. NW, Washington, DC 20049; phone: 202-434-2277).

Golden Companions (PO Box 754, Pullman, WA 99163-0754; phone: 208-858-2183).

Mature Outlook (Customer Service Center, 6001 N. Clark St., Chicago, IL 60660; phone: 800-336-6330).

National Council of Senior Citizens (1331 F St. NW, Washington, DC 20004; phone: 202-347-8800; fax: 202-624-9595).

Package Tour Operators

Elderhostel (75 Federal St., Boston, MA 02110-1941; phone: 617-426-7788; fax: 617-426-8351).

Evergreen Travel Service (4114 198th St. SW, Suite 13, Lynnwood, WA 98036-6742; phone: 800-435-2288 or 206-776-1184; fax: 206-775-0728).

Gadabout Tours (700 E. Tahquitz Canyon Way, Palm Springs, CA 92262; phone: 800-952-5068 or 619-325-5556; fax: 619-325-5127).

Grand Circle Travel (347 Congress St., Boston, MA 02210; phone: 800-221-2610 or 617-350-7500; fax: 617-423-0445).

Grandtravel (6900 Wisconsin Ave., Suite 706, Chevy Chase, MD 20815; phone: 800-247-7651 or 301-986-0790; fax: 301-913-0166).

Interhostel (*University of New Hampshire,* Division of Continuing Education, 6 Garrison Ave., Durham, NH 03824; phone: 800-733-9753 or 603-862-1147; fax: 603-862-1113).

OmniTours (104 Wilmot Rd., Deerfield, IL 60015; phone: 800-962-0060 or 708-374-0088; fax: 708-374-9515).

Saga International Holidays (222 Berkeley St., Boston, MA 02116; phone: 800-343-0273 or 617-262-2262; fax: 617-375-5950).

Money Matters

CURRENCY

Although Bermuda uses US currency as its official means of exchange, the actual currency of the island is the Bermuda dollar (BD$), which is divided into 100 cents. It is pegged to the US dollar (1BD$ = 1US$). US currency is accepted at par at most commercial establishments.

CREDIT CARDS AND TRAVELER'S CHECKS

Most major credit cards enjoy wide domestic and international acceptance. However, not every hotel, restaurant, or shop in Bermuda accepts all (or in some cases any) credit cards. When making purchases with a credit card, also note that most credit card companies charge a 1% fee for converting foreign currency charges to dollars. It's also wise to carry traveler's checks while on the road, since they are widely accepted and replaceable if stolen or lost. You can buy traveler's checks at banks and some are available by mail or phone. Keep a separate list of all traveler's checks (noting those that you have cashed) and the names and numbers of your credit cards. Both traveler's check and credit card companies have international numbers to call for information or in the event of loss or theft.

CASH MACHINES

Automated teller machines (ATMs) are increasingly common worldwide, and most banks participate in international ATM networks such as *CIRRUS* (phone: 800-4-CIRRUS) and *PLUS* (phone: 800-THE-PLUS). Cardholders can withdraw cash from any machine in the same network using either a "bank" card or, in some cases, a credit card. Additional information on ATMs and networks can be obtained from your bank or credit card company. (At press time, all ATM machines in Bermuda were connected to the *PLUS* system and were available only at branches of the Bank of Bermuda.)

SENDING MONEY ABROAD

Note that at the time of this writing, the two major wire services through which money can be sent overseas—*American Express MoneyGram* (phone: 800-926-9400 or 800-666-3997 for information; 800-866-8800 for money transfers) and *Western Union Financial Services* (phone: 800-325-4176)— do not provide service to Bermuda; call for current information when planning your trip. At present, the only way to wire money to Bermuda is through a US bank; contact your local bank branch for instructions. If you are down to your last cent and have no other way to obtain cash, the nearest *US Consulate* will let you call home to set these matters in motion.

Accommodations

For specific information on hotels, resorts, and other selected accommodations see *Best on the Island* in THE ISLAND. Also consult the *Bermuda Department of Tourism*'s publication *Where to Stay in Bermuda*.

RENTAL OPTIONS

An attractive accommodations alternative for visitors content to stay in one spot is to rent one of the numerous properties available throughout Bermuda. For a family or group, the per-person cost can be reasonable. To have your pick of the properties available, make inquiries at least six months in advance. The *Worldwide Home Rental Guide* (369 Montezuma, Suite 338, Santa Fe, NM 87501; phone: 505-984-7080; fax: 505-989-7381) lists rental properties and managing agencies.

Rental Property Agents

Hideaways International (PO Box 4433, Portsmouth, NH 03802-4433; phone: 800-843-4433 or 603-430-4433; fax: 603-430-4444).

Property Rentals International (1 Park W. Circle, Suite 108, Midlothian, VA 23113; phone: 800-220-3332 or 804-378-6054; fax: 804-379-2073).

Rent a Home International (7200 34th Ave. NW, Seattle, WA 98117; phone: 206-789-9377; fax: 206-789-9379).

Rent a Vacation Everywhere (*RAVE*; 383 Park Ave., Rochester, NY 14607; phone: 716-256-0760; fax: 716-256-2676).

VHR Worldwide (235 Kensington Ave., Norwood, NJ 07648; phone: 201-767-9393 in New Jersey; 800-633-3284 elsewhere in the US; fax: 201-767-5510).

Villas International (605 Market St., Suite 510, San Francisco, CA 94105; phone: 800-221-2260 or 415-281-0910; fax: 415-281-0919).

ACCOMMODATIONS DISCOUNTS

The following organizations offer discounts of up to 50% on accommodations in Bermuda:

Entertainment Publishing (2125 Butterfield Rd., Troy, MI 48084; phone: 800-477-3234 or 313-637-8400; fax: 313-637-9779).

Hotel Express (4405 Beltwood Pkwy. N., Dallas, TX 75244; phone: 800-866-2015 or 214-991-5482 for information; 800-580-2083 for reservations; fax: 214-770-3575).

International Travel Card (6001 N. Clark St., Chicago, IL 60660; phone: 800-342-0558 or 312-465-8891; fax: 312-764-8066).

Time Zones

The time in Bermuda is always one hour later than in East Coast US cities. Like the US, Bermuda observes daylight saving time from the first Sunday in April to the last Sunday in October and standard time the rest of the year.

Business and Shopping Hours

Businesses usually are open weekdays from 9 AM to 5 or 6 PM; stores also often open for a full day on Saturdays. Most banks are open weekdays from 9:30 AM to 3 PM, and are closed on weekends. On Fridays, the Bank of Bermuda is open from 9:30 AM to 4:30 PM.

Holidays

In Bermuda, the public holidays this year are as follows:

New Year's Day (January 1)
Good Friday (April 14)
Bermuda Day (May 24)
Queen's Official Birthday (third Monday in June; June 19 this year)
Cup Match and Somer's Day (August 3–4)
Labour Day (first Monday in September; September 4 this year)
Remembrance Day (November 11)
Christmas (December 25)
Boxing Day (December 26)

Mail

When sending mail between the US and Bermuda, always use airmail and allow at least 7 days for delivery. Stamps are available at post offices, most hotel desks, and public vending machines. If your correspondence is especially important, you may want to send it via an international courier service, such as *Federal Express* or *DHL Worldwide Express*.

You can have mail sent to you care of your hotel (marked "Guest Mail, Hold for Arrival") or to a post office (the address should include "c/o General Delivery"). *American Express* offices also will hold mail for customers ("c/o Client Letter Service"); information is provided in their pamphlet *Travelers' Companion*. Note that *US Embassies* and *Consulates* abroad will hold mail for US citizens *only* in emergency situations.

Telephone

Direct dialing is possible between Bermuda and the US.

To call a number in Bermuda from the US: Dial 1 + 809 (the area code) + the local number.

To call a number in the US from Bermuda: Dial 1 + the area code + the local number.

To make a call in Bermuda: Dial the local number.

To reach a local or international operator in Bermuda: Dial 0.

For information: Dial 411 for local information; dial 0 for long-distance (overseas) information.

Although you can use a telephone company calling card number on any phone, pay phones that take major credit cards (*American Express, MasterCard, Visa,* and so on) are increasingly common. Also available are combined telephone calling cards/bank credit cards, such as the *AT&T/Universal Card* (PO Box 44167, Jacksonville, FL 32231-4167; phone: 800-423-4343). Other companies offering long distance phone cards (without additional credit card privileges) include *MCI* (323 Third St. SE, Cedar Rapids, IA 52401; phone: 800-444-4444) and *Sprint* (8140 Ward Pkwy., Kansas City, MO 64114; phone: 800-877-4000).

Hotels routinely add surcharges to the cost of phone calls made from their rooms. Long-distance telephone services that help you avoid this added expense are provided by a number of companies, including *AT&T* (AT&T Communications, International Information Service, 635 Grant St., Pittsburgh, PA 15219; phone: 800-874-4000), *MCI* (address above), and *Sprint* (address above). Note that even when you use such long-distance services, some hotels still may charge a fee for line usage.

Other useful resources for travelers include the *AT&T 800 Travel Directory* (to order, call 800-426-8686); the *Toll-Free Travel & Vacation Information Directory* (Pilot Books, 103 Cooper St., Babylon, NY 11702; phone: 516-422-2225; fax: 516-422-2227); and *The Phone Booklet* (Scott American Corporation, PO Box 88, W. Redding, CT 06896; phone: 203-938-2955).

In an emergency: Dial 911, the number for all emergency services; you also can dial 0 for an operator.

Electricity

Like the US, Bermuda uses 110-volt, 60-cycle, alternating current (AC). Appliances running on standard current can be used without adapters or converters.

Staying Healthy

Tourists most often suffer one health problem in Bermuda: sunburn. In addition, when swimming in the ocean, be aware that the undertow (a current running back down the beach after a wave has washed ashore) can knock you down, and riptides (currents running against the tide) can pull you out to sea. Sharks are sometimes found in local waters, but rarely come close to shore. Jellyfish—including the Portuguese man-of-war—also are common, as are eels and sea urchins, and be aware that coral reefs, though beautiful, can be razor sharp.

Should you need medical attention in a non-emergency situation, ask at your hotel for the house physician or for help in reaching a doctor; referrals also are available from the *US Consulate.* Pharmacies are not open around the clock; if you need a prescription filled during off-hours, go directly to a local hospital. **In an emergency:** Go to the emergency room of the nearest hospital, dial the emergency number provided above, or call an operator for assistance.

Be extremely cautious about injections when traveling abroad because reusable syringes and needles may be used, and sterilization procedures sometimes are inadequate. If you have a condition that requires periodic injections, bring a supply of syringes with you or buy disposable syringes at a local pharmacy.

For up-to-date information on current health conditions, call the Centers for Disease Control's *International Travelers' Hotline:* 404-332-4559.

Additional Resources

InterContinental Medical (2720 Enterprise Pkwy., Suite 106, Richmond, VA 23294; phone: 804-527-1094; fax: 804-527-1941).

International Association for Medical Assistance to Travelers (*IAMAT;* 417 Center St., Lewiston, NY 14092; phone: 716-754-4883; and 40 Regal Rd., Guelph, Ontario N1K 1B5, Canada; phone: 519-836-0102; fax: 519-836-3412).

International Health Care Service (440 E. 69th St., New York, NY 10021; phone: 212-746-1601).

International SOS Assistance (PO Box 11568, Philadelphia, PA 19116; phone: 800-523-8930 or 215-244-1500; fax: 215-244-2227).

Medic Alert Foundation (2323 Colorado Ave., Turlock, CA 95382; phone: 800-ID-ALERT or 209-668-3333; fax: 209-669-2495).

TravMed (PO Box 10623, Baltimore, MD 21285-0623; phone: 800-732-5309 or 410-296-5225; fax: 410-825-7523).

Consular Services

The American Services section of the *US Consulate* is a vital source of assistance and advice for US citizens abroad. If you are injured or become seriously ill, the consulate can direct you to sources of medical attention and notify your relatives. If you become involved in a dispute that could lead to legal action, the consulate can recommend a local attorney. In cases of natural disasters or civil unrest, consulates handle the evacuation of US citizens if necessary.

The *US Consulate* in Bermuda is located at Crown Hill, 16 Middle Rd., Devonshire DVO3, Bermuda (phone: 809-295-1342; fax: 809-295-1592).

The *US State Department* operates an automated 24-hour *Citizens' Emergency Center* travel advisory hotline (phone: 202-647-5225). You also can reach a duty officer at this number from 8:15 AM to 10 PM, eastern standard time on weekdays, and from 9 AM to 3 PM on Saturdays. At all other times, call 202-647-4000. For faxed travel warning and other consular information, call 202-647-3000 using the handset on your fax machine; instructions will be provided. With a PC and a modem, you can access the consular affairs electronic bulletin board (phone: 202-647-9225).

Entry Requirements and Customs Regulations

ENTERING BERMUDA

To visit Bermuda for a period of up to 3 months (extendable to 6 months, upon arrival), US citizens need proof of citizenship (passport, birth certificate, or voter registration card), and an official photo ID (a passport fulfills both these requirements), as well as an ongoing or return ticket. Proof of pre-arranged accommodations also may be required. For longer stays, contact the Chief Immigration Officer (*Dept. of Immigration,* Government Administration Building, 30 Parliament St., Hamilton HM-12, Bermuda; phone: 809-295-5151; fax: 809-295-4115).

RETURNING TO THE US

You must declare to the *US Customs* official at the point of entry everything you have acquired in Bermuda. The standard duty-free allowance for US citizens is $400; if your trip is shorter than 48 continuous hours, or you have been outside the US within the previous 30 days, the duty-free allowance is reduced to $25. Families traveling together may make a joint customs declaration.

A flat 10% duty is assessed on the next $1,000 worth of merchandise; additional items are taxed at a variety of rates (see *Tariff Schedules of the United States* in a library or any *US Customs Service* office). Some articles are duty-free only up to certain limits. The $400 allowance includes 1 carton of (200) cigarettes, 100 cigars (not Cuban), and 1 liter of liquor or wine (for those over 21); the $25 allowance includes 10 cigars, 50 cigarettes, and 4 ounces of perfume. Antiques (at least 100 years old) and paintings or drawings done entirely by hand also are duty-free.

With the exception of gifts valued at $50 or less sent directly to the recipient, *all* items shipped home are dutiable. To avoid paying duty unnecessarily on expensive items (such as computer equipment) that you plan to take with you on your trip, register these items with *US Customs* before you depart. Note that US regulations prohibit the import of some goods sold abroad—such as articles made of the furs or hides of animals on the endangered species list.

For further information, consult *Currency Reporting; GSP and the Traveler; Importing a Car; International Mail Imports; Know Before You Go; Pets, Wildlife, US Customs; Pocket Hints;* and *Travelers' Tips on Bringing Food, Plant, and Animal Products into the United States;* all are available from the *US Customs Service* (PO Box 7407, Washington, DC 20044). For tape-recorded information on travel-related topics, call 202-927-2095 from any touch-tone phone.

DUTY-FREE SHOPS

Located in international airports, these provide bargains on the purchase of foreign goods. But beware: Not all foreign goods are automatically less expensive. You *can* get a good deal on some items, but know what they cost elsewhere before making any purchases.

For Further Information

Offices of the *Bermuda Department of Tourism* in the US are the best sources of travel information. These offices generally are open on weekdays, during normal business hours. For information on entry requirements and customs regulations in Bermuda, contact a *British Consulate* or the *British Embassy*'s Consular Section.

Bermuda Department of Tourism

California: c/o *Tetley, Moyer & Associates,* 3151 Cahuenga Blvd. W., Suite 111, Los Angeles CA 90068 (phone: 800-421-0000 or 213-436-0744; fax: 213-436-0750).

Georgia: 245 Peachtree Center Ave. NE, Suite 803, Atlanta, GA 30303 (phone: 404-524-1541; fax: 404-586-9933).

Illinois: 150 N. Wacker Dr., Suite 1070, Chicago, IL 60606 (phone: 312-782-5486; fax: 312-704-6996).

Massachusetts: 44 School St., Suite 1010, Boston, MA 02108 (phone: 617-742-0405).

New York: 310 Madison Ave., Suite 201, New York, NY 10017 (phone: 212-818-9800 in New York City; 800-223-6106 elsewhere in the US; fax: 212-983-5289).

British Embassy and Consulates in the US
Embassy (Consular Section)
Washington, DC: 19 Observatory Circle NW, Washington, DC 20008-3611 (phone: 202-462-1340 or 202-986-0205; fax: 202-797-2929).

Consulates General
California: 11766 Wilshire Blvd., Suite 400, Los Angeles, CA 90025 (phone: 310-477-3322; fax: 310-575-1450).

Georgia: Marquis One Tower, 245 Peachtree Ctr. Ave., Suite 2700, Atlanta, GA 30303 (phone: 404-524-5856; fax: 404-524-3153).

Illinois: 33 N. Dearborn St., Chicago, IL 60602 (phone: 312-346-1810; fax: 312-346-7021).

Massachusetts: Federal Reserve Plaza, 600 Atlantic Ave., 25th floor, Boston, MA 02210 (phone: 617-248-9555; fax: 617-248-9578).

New York: 845 Third Ave., New York, NY 10022 (phone: 212-745-0200; fax: 212-754-3062).

Texas: 1100 Milam Bldg., 1100 Milam, Suite 2260, Houston, TX 77002-5506 (phone: 713-659-6270; fax: 713-659-7094).

The Island

Bermuda

Bermuda is, plain and simple, the quintessential tourist island—a fact inspired as much by necessity as inclination. For the truth is that tourism is Bermuda's most important industry, and an instinct for self-preservation and the recognition of economic reality have manifested themselves in an island population that recognizes how much it depends on tourist traffic.

That Bermuda has probably the highest incidence of return visitors of any resort island—in recent years, an impressive 42%—testifies most dramatically to how well Bermudians do their job. From the taxi driver who describes his island with obvious pride to the shop clerk who sets an all-too-seldom-seen standard of service and helpfulness, Bermudians treat visitors as they would any treasured natural resource. And the almost omnipresent smiles set a tone of friendliness that is hard to resist.

Physically, Bermuda is as pretty as its postcards—maybe prettier. Green hills, white roofs, pastel houses, bright flowers, pink sand beaches, and blue and turquoise seas are all waiting as your plane lands at the airport or your ship glides through Two Rock Passage and into Hamilton Harbour. You can count on Bermuda's beauty, as visitors have since 1779, the year the first known American tourist went to the island for his health.

The first European to set foot on Bermuda arrived several hundred years earlier. Spaniard Juan de Bermúdez is credited with the island's discovery; he stumbled upon it while returning from the Caribbean to Europe in 1503. For the next century or so, Bermuda's only visitors were shipwrecked sailors; those who lived to tell the world about their find painted a picture of an island beset by devils and treacherous waters. While these tales were said to have inspired Shakespeare to set *The Tempest* in Bermuda, they did little to encourage permanent settlement. Then, in 1609, a British ship en route to Jamestown ran aground off what is now St. George's. The captain, Admiral Sir George Somers, and his crew built two new ships from the wreckage and continued their journey, leaving three men behind to explore this new territory. These men—Edward Chase, Robert Waters, and Christopher Carter—were the first permanent residents of Bermuda; some of their descendants still live on the island today. Word that Bermuda was "the richest, healthfullest, and most pleasing land as ever man set foot upon" spread rapidly, and three years later, a group of British settlers led by Governor Richard Moore landed here to officially establish a settlement on St. George's. Conditions were harsh and difficult for the colonists, but they managed to eke out a living, even to the point of building several crude forts to protect themselves. They successfully drove off an invasion attempt by Spain in 1614, and Bermuda has been a Crown Colony ever since.

Although Bermuda itself has been free from invasion, the island has been involved in several other countries' wars. After the American

Revolution, Britain sought to reassert control of the rest of the western Atlantic by shoring up Bermuda's naval installations. During the first half of the 19th century, British convict laborers built the *Royal Naval Dockyard* on Bermuda's Ireland Island and several other forts, which were pressed into service during the War of 1812. About 50 years later, the outbreak of the Civil War in the US embroiled Bermuda once again in naval politics. Many Bermudians supported the Confederacy, sending supplies to the South despite President Abraham Lincoln's embargo.

By the mid-17th century, Bermuda had a flourishing economy. Islanders were making money by selling salt (obtained from the Turks Islands, which was a Bermudian colony) and native and American tobacco, as well as by building ships from sturdy local cedar. After the British annexed the Turks Islands in 1799, the Bermudian merchants shrewdly made up for their loss of the salt trade by obtaining permission from Elias Haskett, the free-wheeling Governor of the Bahamas, to attack pirates roaming the northern Caribbean and appropriate their cargoes. At that time, however, the island's economic success was tainted by the specter of slavery: Beginning in the 1640s, blacks, native Indians, and Irish and Scottish indentured servants were shipped here and put to work. Conditions were often cruel, and slaves were subject to unfair restrictions (one law required that a black person meeting a white Bermudian after sunset drop to his or her knees or be punished with 100 lashes). After several uprisings, slavery was abolished in 1834.

By the late 19th century, the island discovered a new and more profitable trade: tourism. In 1882, Queen Victoria's daughter, Louise, the wife of Canada's governor-general, landed on the island for a much-publicized winter visit. Three years later, the 100-room *Hamilton Princess* hotel, with its double-tiered verandahs overlooking the harbor, was built just outside Hamilton and named in her honor. Bermuda became a fashionable vacation destination; many celebrated figures came, including Mark Twain, who visited frequently between 1867 and 1910. Other industries gradually took hold as well, including trade in such agricultural products as Bermuda onions, potatoes, carrots, and *Easter* lilies. In addition, shipping firms, trading and investment companies, and insurance houses began to establish headquarters here, attracted by the island's low taxes and minimal bureaucracy. But by the mid-20th century, tourism was the mainstay of Bermuda's economy.

As the island's wealth increased over the past 50 years, so have calls for independence. Although Bermudians have elected to remain subjects of the queen, they've acquired more local autonomy. Political parties have emerged, notably the conservative United Bermuda Party, which has controlled Bermuda's parliament and administration in modern times, and the Progressive Labour Party, which derives its strength from the colony's industrial unions. Racial tensions (60% of the Bermudian population is black) are not unknown on the island, but they are rare enough to pass unnoticed by the visitor.

In 21 square miles of islands (Bermuda's myriad isles are joined by causeways and bridges, and often are not easily distinguishable), there isn't room for two worlds—one for tourists and one for locals—so Bermudians and visitors share a lot. They buy their Shetland sweaters and tennis balls at the same shops, play on the same golf courses, have Sunday brunch and Thursday dinner at the same restaurants. They sail the same waters and watch the same soccer matches. They enjoy the same unhurried sense of leisure and love the same scenery. For visitors, these are vacation pluses. For Bermudians, they're essentials for everyday life—and worth protecting.

Although the 20th century has definitely made its mark, Bermuda, which is a self-governing British colony, still clings to its charming old ways. Cars still drive on the left (the speed limit is posted at 20 mph), and the number of motor vehicles on the island is limited—though there are still too many of them for the narrow, twisting coral-walled lanes, especially now that so many taxi cabs are mini-vans. Hotel building is carefully monitored because island administrators feel it's essential to keep their hills and beaches from becoming crowded. Building codes are carefully enforced, so no high-rise hotels block views or beget shadows that block out the sun. A 20th-century cottage is likely to bear a strong resemblance to its 17th-century neighbor or—even more likely—to be a house built between then and now and recently restored. Neon signs are still strictly forbidden; in fact, even additional traffic lights in Hamilton are likely to cause enough furor to merit the attention of the *Bermuda National Trust.* And legalized gambling, says one official, is "most unlikely in this century or the next." Even the occasional rousing rainstorm or hurtling hurricane fails to fluster the local calm.

There will, however, continue to be all manner of first class places to stay on Bermuda, and the service is sure to stay friendly and efficient. Visitors are still certain to find fine golf courses and tennis courts that need not be booked days in advance (except perhaps for weekends), and pink beaches that–magically—never seem to get too crowded. Here, it seems, there always will be green hills and white roofs and pink cottages with herb-bordered gardens and palm trees. And clear nights when the smell of jasmine and cedar smoke fills the air. And a way of life that sends you home restored—longing to return.

On Bermuda, thanks mostly to the Bermudians, you can count on it.

Bermuda At-a-Glance

FROM THE AIR

Just 21 miles long and, for most of its length, barely a half mile wide, Bermuda is a fishhook-shaped chain of nearly 150 islands and about the same number of islets—at some points linked by bridges you don't even notice as you cross—anchored in the Atlantic Ocean about 600 miles due east of Cape Hatteras, North Carolina. Composed of lava, coral, and limestone (of which most Bermudian homes are built), it is based on the summit of a long-extinct volcano.

At the islands' western end, the bight of the "fishhook" curves protectively around Little Sound and Great Sound, at the eastern end of which is the city of Hamilton, capital of the colony and its chief cruise port. The airport at Kindley Field is about 14 miles northeast of Hamilton, at the western edge of the much larger US Naval Air Station.

The colony's most famous and photographed beaches lie along the islands' southern edge, and their fine, soft coral sand is actually tinged with pink. Many visitors are surprised that Bermuda has very few indigenous palm trees; that's because its climate is subtropical rather than tropical. And although much of it is green and rolling, it has no rivers or streams. It depends almost entirely on rainfall for its freshwater supply; water is caught by the whitewashed roofs of its houses, and stored in cistern tanks below ground. (To a Bermudian home owner, the size of his cistern is often a greater source of pride than the size of the house itself.)

The Olde Towne of St. George's—Bermuda's first capital and second city—sits at the far eastern tip of the islands. Colonized in 1612 by members of the Virginia Company after the islands' unplanned settlement in 1609 by Sir George Somers and his shipwrecked crew, it is the site of considerable restoration, exemplified by the *Somers Wharf* shopping area. Cruise ships call here, as well as in Hamilton and at the historic *Royal Naval Dockyard* (also known simply as the *Dockyard*), with its complex of shops and a crafts market, at the western end of the islands (for more information see *Stepping Out in Sandys* in DIRECTIONS).

The best place to begin a tour is at the visitors' service bureau, in Hamilton, which is next to the ferry terminal near Front Street's west end (see *Tourist Information*).

SPECIAL PLACES

HAMILTON The colony's capital city is a pretty, pastel and white town on the inner shore (and close to the center) of the island fishhook, at the eastern end of Bermuda's Great Sound. It's the very exceptional visitor who doesn't come here at least once to shop, to wash down the spicy Bermuda fish chowder with a pint in one of its pubs, and perhaps even to take a horse-drawn carriage ride. Many never make it farther than Front Street, the main street that runs along to the water's edge from Bermudiana Road at its west end to King Street in the east. And it's fair to say that you won't be culturally disadvantaged if you don't either. Still, a walking tour of the town's landmarks takes little more than an hour, and provides some interesting background on local history and government. For a detailed look at Hamilton, see *Passing Through Pembroke and the City of Hamilton* in DIRECTIONS.

ELSEWHERE ON THE ISLAND

Outside the capital, principal sightseeing routes head east and west from one of two traffic rotaries (called roundabouts here) south and southeast of the city (for more information on walking and biking tours, see DIRECTIONS).

To reach the first roundabout, bear right on Crow Lane at the end of Front Street. At the circle, you can go three-quarters of the way around, peel off to the right at The Lane, then go right on Harbour Road for a purely scenic bike ride along the water (detour at snapshot-worthy Salt Kettle). Go past the Belmont Wharf to Burnt House Hill and then on to Middle Road.

Or leave the first roundabout halfway around and turn up Trimingham Road to a second traffic circle, off which you can go west or east on the South Road.

SOUTH ROAD WEST On the road west toward Somerset are the island's most beautiful beaches (at Warwick Long, Jobson, Stonehole, Chaplin, and Horseshoe Bays). Just beyond the *Princess* golf course (on the right), turn right up Lighthouse Road to the world's second-oldest cast-iron lighthouse, opened in 1847. There's an admission charge to climb to the top for a 360° view; the climb takes 5 minutes, with rest areas along the way. Those who forego the trip to the top still can enjoy a grand view from the lighthouse base. Back on South Road, pass Church Bay to join the Middle Road, which skirts the *Port Royal* golf course, crosses Somerset Bridge (the world's narrowest drawbridge, with a "flap" just wide enough to let a sailboat mast pass through), and becomes Somerset Road. At this point, Ely's Harbour and Cathedral Rocks are on your left. For more information, see *Stepping Out in Sandys* in DIRECTIONS.

SOUTH ROAD EAST The road east from the Trimingham Road roundabout toward the Olde Towne of St. George's passes the *Botanical Gardens of Bermuda* and *Camden* (phone: 236-5732), a restored house that now serves as the official home of Bermuda's premier, the Honorable Sir John Swan (also see *Historic Homes and Gardens* and *Natural Wonderlands* in DIVERSIONS). *Camden* is open to the public (unless an official function is being held) on Tuesday and Friday afternoons. No admission charge. The road forks about 2 miles from here. Continue east to Spittal Pond, 50 acres of woodland and meadows and the site of Bermuda's largest wildlife sanctuary. Then stop at *Verdmont* (phone: 236-7369), an 18th-century *Bermuda National Trust* home with gardens and antiques. Closed Sundays. Admission charge. (For more information, see *Historic Homes and Gardens* in DIVERSIONS.) Farther along this route is *Devil's Hole Aquarium* (phone: 293-2072), offering hookless fishing—fun for kids, dull for grown-ups. Open daily. Admission charge. Also worth visiting are *Leamington Caves* (no phone); and *Crystal Caves* (phone: 293-0640), which some say are the prettier of the two. Both caves are open daily and charge admission. Take Harrington Sound Road to North Shore Road and cross into Hamilton Parish, where you can stop for refreshments at the *Swizzle Inn* (phone: 293-9300) or *Bailey's Ice Cream Parlour* (see *Eating Out* for the latter); once refreshed, visit the nearby *Bermuda Perfumery* and mini-botanical garden (North Shore Rd.; phone: 293-0627). Perfume is made here, and passionflowers grow like grapes on vines outside (closed Sundays during winter). A possible detour (especially if you're hungry for fish): Turn right on St. David's Road to visit century-old *St. David's Lighthouse,* from which Bermudians keep watch for *Newport–Bermuda Ocean Yacht Race* winners, and funky *Dennis's Hideaway,* where Dennis Lamb spins Bermudian yarns as he cooks up a moderately priced seafood banquet known as "the works" in his shanty café; call him ahead of time (phone: 297-0044). If you pass up the detour, it's on to the Olde Towne. For more information on these routes, see *Paget Pleasures, Sauntering in Smith's,* and *Hiking Through Hamilton* in DIRECTIONS.

EXTRA SPECIAL

St. George's, Bermuda's first capital, founded in 1612, is the focus of considerable thoughtful restoration. It offers several intriguing old sites: great, gray *Fort St. Catherine,* with historic dioramas and replicas of Britain's crown jewels; *St. Peter's Church,* the oldest Anglican place of worship in the Western Hemisphere; the handsome 1620 *State House,* for which a one-peppercorn rent is handed over with great ceremony every April; and museums full of carriages and Confederate memorabilia. For more information, see *Strolling St. George's* in DIRECTIONS.

Sources and Resources

TOURIST INFORMATION

In Bermuda, the main office of the *Bermuda Department of Tourism* is at *Global House* (43 Church St., Hamilton; phone: 292-0023). There are visitors' service bureaus on Front Street near Albuoy's Point where the ferry docks in Hamilton (phone: 295-1480); at the airport in the arrivals hall; on King's Square opposite the *Town Hall* in St. George's (phone: 297-1642); and at the *Dockyard* (phone: 234-3824). All are open daily.

LOCAL COVERAGE *This Week in Bermuda, Bermuda Weekly,* and *Preview of Bermuda* all provide general tourist information, details on sightseeing and sports, up-to-date hotel entertainment schedules, and restaurant listings. Also helpful are the *Handy Reference Map, Welcome to Hamilton, Welcome to the West End, Welcome to St. George's,* and the *Bermuda Railway Trail,* all available at visitors' service bureaus. The *Bermuda Book Store* (see *Shopping*) stocks the latest books about Bermuda. Dial 974 on any local phone for a schedule of the day's happenings, 977 for the weather, and 909 for time and temperature. Tune to radio station VSB—1160 and 1280 AM—for daily tourism broadcasting.

The *Royal Gazette* is the daily paper; the *Bermuda Sun* and the *Mid Ocean News* are published on Fridays. The *Bermuda Times* is published on Wednesdays. *Dining Out in Bermuda* ($3) is invaluable, with more than 50 reproduced menus from the islands' top dining spots. The magazine-format book is available in local shops.

At St. George's, see *The Bermuda Journey,* an audiovisual show depicting 375 years of the islands' history and heritage. It's closed Sundays and public holidays. Admission charge.

For background reading, try *The Caribbean: The Land and its Peoples* by Eintou Springer (Silver Burdett Press; $16.98). You also might want to reread *The Tempest,* said to have been set in Shakespeare's fantasy version of Bermuda.

TELEPHONE The area code for Bermuda is 809.

GETTING AROUND

BUGGY RIDE The traditional Bermuda buggy ride, in a one- or two-horse–drawn carriage, is sentimental, a shade corny—and fun (every honeymoon should include one). Rides are usually a half-hour long; if you've no place special in mind, the driver will probably tour Hamilton and its suburbs (including the one they call Fairylands). Arrangements for night rides should be made in advance. Drivers congregate on Front Street near the flagpole and the cruise ship docks.

BICYCLE RENTAL Pedal bikes (as they're called in Bermuda—mopeds are called bikes here) are best suited to touring around Hamilton or the *Dockyard* or parts of the old Railway Trail, particularly in the island's western environs. For three-speed or 10-gear mountain bikes, contact *Ray's Cycles Ltd.* (Middle Rd., Southampton West; phone: 234-0629; at the *Lantana Colony Club;* Somerset Bridge, Somerset; phone: 234-0141; and at the *Dockyard* for ship passengers; phone: 234-2764); and *Wheels Limited* (Dundonald St., Hamilton; phone: 295-0112; and Devil's Hole; phone: 293-1280).

BUS Painted pink with a dark blue stripe, buses cover all major routes on the island. Bus stop marker poles are also painted pink and blue. Service is efficient and follows regular daytime schedules. The islands are divided into 14 zones. Fare is $3 per adult for an islandwide bus ride; $1.50 within up to three zones; children ages 3 to 12 pay 65¢, which covers all zones; children under 3 travel free. Exact change is required; three- and seven-day passes are available. Buses leave from the *Central Terminal* on Washington Street, just off Church Street and a few steps east of Hamilton's *City Hall.* Route 1 goes from Hamilton to *Marriott's Castle Harbour* and, less frequently, St. George's via John Smith's Bay; Route 3, Hamilton to the *Grotto Bay Beach* hotel via Devil's Hole and the caves; Route 6, from St. George's to St. David's; Route 7, from Hamilton to the *Sonesta Beach* hotel via the South Shore beaches and from Hamilton to the *Dockyard* and the *Maritime Museum* via South

Shore; Route 8, Hamilton to Barnes Corner, Southampton, via Middle Road and the *Southampton Princess*, and to the *Dockyard* and the *Maritime Museum;* and Routes 10 and 11, from Hamilton to St. George's via the aquarium and the *Bermuda Perfumery.* Route 1 to St. George's is more scenic, passing the splendid homes of Tucker's Town; it takes about 10 minutes longer than Routes 10 and 11. If you leave for St. George's from the West End, ask for a free transfer; you'll change buses at Hamilton. For further information on routes and schedules, call 292-3851.

CAR RENTAL Visitors cannot rent (or drive) a car in Bermuda. Because of the island's small size, officials strictly limit the number of cars to only one per household.

FERRY SERVICES The best seagoing buy on the island is a ride on one of the Bermudian government ferries that crisscross the Great Sound and Hamilton Harbour, with stops at Hamilton, Paget, Warwick, and Somerset (see *Taking to the Water* in DIVERSIONS). You can use the ferry dock for much more than just point-to-point transportation, since a waterborne perspective (easily acquired on a once-around-the-harbor ride) provides real insight into Bermuda's oceangoing lifestyle. Sample one-way fares: Hamilton to Paget and Warwick, $1.50; Hamilton to Somerset, $3. Pedal bikes ride at no charge; mopeds may be carried on the Somerset ferry (at the captain's discretion) for $3. For information, call 295-4506.

MOPED RENTAL Years before the US discovered the moped, this motor-assisted bicycle became Bermuda's tourists' favorite means of transport. Bike liveries are handy to most hotels, and once or twice around the parking lot is generally enough to give you the hang of driving one. Though you can rent bikes (mopeds) with pillions (that's the extra seat behind) if there are two of you, two bikes are better than one for safety and maneuverability. Rates include third-party insurance, lock, basket, helmet, delivery and collection (which can be arranged in advance), and breakdown service (during working hours). If your hotel doesn't have its own bike rental setup, somebody at the desk will be happy to make arrangements; delivery is usually possible within an hour. Or contact *Wheels Limited* (see *Bicycle Rental,* above); *Oleander Cycle* (Valley Rd., Paget; phone: 236-5235; and Gorham Rd., Hamilton; phone: 295-0919); *Ray's Cycles Ltd.* (see *Bicycle Rental,* above); *St. George's Cycle Livery* (Water St., St. George's; phone: 297-1463); or *Honda Rentals* (Front St., Hamilton; phone: 292-3775 or 292-6853). *Rockford Cycles* (Glebe Rd., Pembroke; phone: 292-1534) and *Smatt's Cycle Livery* (at the *Hamilton Princess* hotel, Pitt's Bay; phone: 295-1180) rent single- and double-seat mopeds as well as scooters. Mopeds may be taken on ferries for a small fee.

Bermuda is just the right size for mopeding. You can get from Hamilton to St. George's in the east or Somerset in the west in 30 to 45 minutes; but visitors hardly move that far or that fast in a day. Of all the trails cyclists can take (equestrians and pedestrians, too), the most fun is the paved Bermuda Railway Trail (see *Wandering Warwick* in DIRECTIONS), which follows the route the railroad took before cars were introduced in 1946; the best stretch for scooters is from the Somerset bus terminal to Somerset Bridge, and from Whale Bay Road's entrance to Frank's Bay, Southampton. The key to a safe moped or bicycle rental on Bermuda is to keep mumbling to yourself (especially at the roundabouts), "Keep left and don't look back." Also remember that it's illegal to bike without a helmet, and most gas stations (except those at marinas) are closed Sundays.

SEA EXCURSIONS All sorts of craft—cruisers, glass-bottom boats, catamarans, and yachts—take off from Hamilton Harbour in all directions. Some also have expanded operations to the *Dockyard* at the West End. Among the best are the all-day classic offered by *Bermuda Island Cruises* (phone: 292-8652), which includes lunch, a swizzle party, continuous commentary, and stops in St. George's and the *Dockyard;* and the morning and afternoon boat trips to the *Sea Gardens* that are given from April to November by *Bermuda Water Tours* (phone: 295-3727). The best snorkeling and glass-bottom boat cruise (including instruction and equipment) is run by *Pitman's Snorkeling* (phone: 234-0700).

SIGHTSEEING BUS TRIPS Although taxi touring is much more fun and more flexible, there are some decent bus tours available. One good tour operator is *St. George's Transportation and Scenic Tours* (phone: 297-8492), which offers tours of the island and the East End from April through November.

TAXI They meet every flight and cruise ship. All are metered and carry four to six people. Drivers are cheerful and courteous and very well informed. (Taxis can be expensive if you don't share your ride with a lot of people–standard rates are $4 for the first mile and $1.40 for each additional mile.) To summon a cab by telephone, call 295-4141 or 292-4476. For the South Shore and points west, a less expensive alternative is to share a limousine from the airport. Contact *Bermuda Hosts, Ltd.* (phone: 293-1334) or *Beeline Transportation* (phone: 293-0303). If you arrive in Bermuda with no transportation, check to see if a waiting limo has room for you.

TAXI TOURING Drivers with small blue flags on their cabs have passed special exams to qualify as tour guides; they're almost always most informative and a pleasure to have as guides. Among our favorites are Vince Cann (phone: 236-3040, home; 234-7346, car); Custerfield Crockwell (phone: 297-1001, home; 234-8014, car); and Victor Woolridge (phone: 236-9274, home; 234-8896, car), who was recognized by Queen Elizabeth during her 1975 visit to the island for his contributions to tourism. When you discuss the route, let the driver know if you're interested in taking pictures; he knows the best vantage points. *Meyer Agencies* (phone: 295-4176) offers several tours, including a three-hour trip to Harrington Sound, a four-hour Somerset tour, and a five-hour St. George's Island tour.

SPECIAL EVENTS

In addition to the sports competitions for which Bermuda is famous (sailing race weeks, tennis weeks, international game fishing, golf tournaments, an international marathon, 10K races, and triathlons), Bermuda has a host of year-round activities. The stellar, annual *Bermuda Festival,* which takes place during most of January and February, attracts top names in theater, music, and dance. In April and May, private houses and gardens are open to the public on Wednesday afternoons; daylong tours are given by the *Garden Club of Bermuda. Bermuda Day* (May 24), the highlight of *Heritage Month,* is celebrated with the *Heritage Parade,* a mini-marathon, Bermuda sailboat races, and exhibits of island art and culture; it's also the day it becomes socially acceptable for Bermudians to go swimming. *Somers Day* is actually a two-day holiday (usually the Thursday and Friday before the first Monday in August) featuring the annual *Cup Match Cricket Festival* between the *St. George's* and *Somerset* teams (see *Sports and Fitness*). At *Christmastime,* the mayor's welcome takes place in St. George's; the Gombey dancers can be seen strutting their stuff around the island; and a stirring skirling ceremony can be seen and heard at Fort Hamilton (see *Quintessential Bermuda* in DIVERSIONS for the latter two).

MUSEUMS

The best thing about the island's museums is that they are easy and fun to peruse. They are easy because they are not monolithic; they can be slipped into and out of as comfortably as the sea, and they can offer an interesting hour's diversion when the rain falls, when the beach is just a touch too crowded, or when the day's lunch still weighs heavily. And they are fun because in that hour you will assimilate more than you ever thought possible about island history and culture.

BERMUDA MARITIME MUSEUM Though rather remotely situated on Ireland Island, it offers a formidable display of sea treasures in a unique setting. Located in an old dockyard and housed in the building where the munitions of the Royal Navy were once guarded, this museum not only offers a collection of full-scale and model ships, but also has nautical relics and equipment, charts, prints, paintings, maps, and whaling gear illustrating Bermuda's connection with the sea. Also on display are some of Bermudian deep-sea diver Teddy Tucker's collection of underwater treasures, and exhibits on the history of diving. There is also an informal restaurant. Open daily. Admission charge. Ireland Island, Somerset (phone: 234-1418).

MASTERWORKS FOUNDATION GALLERY On exhibit here are oils, lithographs, and a large collection of watercolors done by visiting artists between 1815 and the 1950s, including works by well-known French cubist Albert Gleizes and Americans George Ault and Ogden Pleissner. Closed Sunday afternoons; hours may vary depending on volunteer availability. Donation suggested. 97 Front St., Hamilton (phone: 295-5580).

NATIONAL ART GALLERY Housed in the East Exhibition Room of *City Hall* in Hamilton, it boasts a collection of European art dating from the 15th to the 19th centuries, plus the works of other international and Bermudian artists. The main level houses the Ondaaj Wing, dedicated to historical works—among them pieces from the National Archives and the *Bermuda National Trust.* Open daily. Admission charge. *City Hall,* Hamilton (phone: 295-9428).

The island's beauty is also reflected in the works of many Bermudian artists; their diverse creations make for lasting reminders of your visit. A few market their work directly; others sell theirs through the *Windjammer Gallery* and *Heritage House* in Hamilton (see *Shopping,* below) and *Bridge House Gallery* (phone: 297-8211) in St. George's. The following is a list of local artists and the galleries where their original work is sold:

Joan Forbes exhibits and sells her watercolors, lithographs, silk-screen and block prints, and oils from *Art House,* her studio on South Road, Paget (near the *Paraquet* restaurant). The studio is open by appointment only during January and February; daily the rest of the year (phone: 236-6746).

Alfred Birdsey creates French Impressionist–style watercolors and lithographs (using stone plates) in his studio at Stowe Hill, Paget. It's closed Sundays (phone: 236-6658).

Carole Holding's watercolors are sold at three outlets: the *Clock Tower* building at the *Dockyard* (phone: 234-3800), which is open daily; and in St. George's at *Featherbed Alley* (phone: 297-1833) and *Long House* at Meyer's Wharf (phone: 297-2354). Both St. George's locations are closed Sundays. Desmond Fountain's lifelike bronze sculptures—seen at hotels and parks throughout the island—are sold from his studio, which is open by appointment only (phone: 292-3955), or the *Sculpture Gallery* (at the *Southampton Princess* hotel; phone: 238-8840), which is closed Sundays.

Jaqui Murray-Hall exhibits and sells her work—depictions of animals in a variety of media—at the *Bermuda Arts Centre* in the *Dockyard;* the center is closed Mondays through Wednesdays from January through April. Contact either the arts center (phone: 234-3361) or Murray-Hall herself (phone: 238-1920).

SHOPPING

It's a high-quality operation all the way; even standard souvenirs look less tacky here than they do in other parts of the world. There are some substantial bargains to be found, especially on imported British goods like woolens (men's sportswear, blazers, kilts, bolts of tartan, tweeds) and Shetland sweaters. Be sure to check the label: "made in Hong Kong" isn't British. The absence of a sales tax in Bermuda means added savings. Fine china and crystal are available at 40% less than in major US cities. Other worthwhile buys: Harris tweed jackets, at about half the going US price; French perfume; and some cosmetics at 30% below stateside prices. Liquor is 25% to 40% less expensive than back home, so you save even when you buy more than your one-liter-per-person duty-free allowance. US duty on wines is nominal—well under $1 per liter even for fortified wines, sparkling wines, and champagne—so if you know your wines and your stateside prices, you can save here, too. Remember to shop early—at least 24 hours before you leave—to allow time for delivery of in-bond goods to your plane or ship.

Though there are some authentic Bermuda antiques for sale, Bermudians are extremely reluctant to let them leave the colony. You can, however, find excellent buys in British antiques even when you add in the cost of shipping and insurance. There is no US duty on any piece over 100 years old. *Trimingham's, H. A. & E. Smith, Bluck's,* and *Heritage House* (see listings below) are specialists in antiques and good reproductions, as are *Timeless Antiques* (Church St.; phone: 295-5008) and *Thistle Gallery* (Park Rd.; phone: 292-3839) in Hamilton.

Among Bermuda's products, Outerbridge's Sherry Peppers Sauce (to spice up your own chowder, soup, and Bloody Marys); delicious Bermuda honey; *Fourways Inn*'s "Dark 'n' Stormy" cakes; Horton's Bermuda rum cake; Bermuda Gold loquat liqueur; Gosling's bottled Bermuda rum swizzle; and the Royall Lyme line of men's after-shave lotions and soaps are standouts. Bermuda-made perfume isn't all that exciting.

Most stores in Hamilton, St. George's, and Somerset are open Mondays through Saturdays from 9 AM to 5:30 or 6 PM, but several open at 9:15 AM and close as early as 5 PM. Some stores are open evenings and Sundays when cruise ships are in port. For last-minute purchases, it's worth noting that hotel branches of stores often are open later or on Sundays, when their Hamilton headquarters are not. When the ships are in Hamilton, try less crowded Somerset and St. George's stores for shopping. Prices are the same, though the shops and selections are smaller.

For general shopping, start with Front Street's Big Three:

A. S. Cooper & Sons Top-quality British-cut sportswear including Austin Reed blazers for men, and European fashions and Indonesian batik cotton clothing for women. Fine collections of crystal and china (Wedgwood, Waterford, Belleek, Lladró, Swarovski), French perfume, and more (phone: 295-3961). There's a branch on *Somers Wharf* in St. George's (phone: 297-0925) and in all the major hotels.

H. A. & E. Smith For big names in British sportswear (including large sizes), Burberry rainwear, Church's English designer shoes, its own private-label apparel, tartans by the yard, and a rather large selection of classy gifts (porcelain placecard holders, pomander balls, Bermuda scarves, china flower pins, earrings, and paperweights) for less than you'd expect (phone: 295-2288). There is a branch in St. George's (York St.; phone: 297-1734) and others in the *Southampton Princess* hotel (on Middle Rd. near Riddell's Bay; phone:

238-0766) and the *Belmont* hotel (overlooking Hamilton Harbour; same phone as main store).

Trimingham's For classic men's and women's fashions, sweaters, and woolens; Hermès and Liberty of London silk scarves; European and British crystal and china; locally crafted gold jewelry; plus perfume and miscellaneous knickknacks. In addition to its two Front Street locations (phone: 295-1183 for both), it has branches in the major hotels; on *Somers Wharf* in St. George's (phone: 297-1726); in Somerset (two locations: Somerset Village; phone: 234-1879; and Mangrove Bay Rd.; phone: 234-1744); and on South Road in Paget (phone: 236-7712).

In addition, these other Hamilton stores are worth looking into (Front Street is the major shopping magnet):

Archie Brown & Son British sportswear for men, women, and children, Braemar sweaters, Pringle cashmeres, and a large selection of tartan items. If you're up to it, they also have Fair Isle sweater kits so you can knit your own. A large children's department also offers toys and books. Front St. (phone: 295-2928).

Aston & Gunn This emporium features custom-made clothing and accessories for men, fine international women's fashions, and designer labels for men and women. Reid St. (phone: 295-4866).

Astwood-Dickinson Fine jewelry and the largest collection of Swiss watches on the island. Six locations: two on Front St. (phone: 292-5805 and 292-4247); Queen St. (phone: 295-5462); the *Hamilton Princess* hotel (Pitt's Bay; phone: 295-0419); the *Southampton Princess* hotel (on Middle Rd. near Riddell's Bay; phone: 238-0448); and the *Sonesta Beach* hotel (Southampton; phone: 238-1976).

Bermuda Book Store The place for paperbacks and books about Bermuda. In a wonderful old building on Queen St. (phone: 295-3698).

Bermuda Coin & Stamp Company Sets of Bermudian and British coins from antique gold doubloons to new decimal coins; specializes in Bermuda philatelic items. Before buying, check US regulations on importing gold. Up Old Cellar La., off Front St. (phone: 295-5503).

Bermuda Railway Company A subsidiary of *Trimingham's,* it carries a line of men's and women's cotton sportswear. Five locations: Reid St. (phone: 295-4830); Mangrove Bay Rd., Somerset (phone: 234-3169); South Rd., Paget (phone: 236-3356); Kings Sq., St. George's (phone: 297-0546); and at *Crystal Cave,* Wilkinson Ave., Hamilton Parish (phone: 293-0942).

Bluck's Lots of china, silver, and some very nice antiques. On Front St. West (phone: 295-5367). Branches on Queen St. (phone: 295-3894); Water St., St. George's (phone: 297-0476); at the *Clock Tower, Dockyard* (phone: 234-

3775); in the *Southampton Princess* hotel (on Middle Rd. near Riddell's Bay; phone: 238-0992); and at the *Sonesta Beach* hotel (Southampton; phone: 238-1440).

Calypso High-fashion European sportswear for women, unusual costume jewelry, the island's largest selection of swimwear, and Joan & David shoes at 10% less than US prices. Bermuda's only outlet for Louis Vuitton luggage and accessories. Front St. (phone: 295-2112). Branches in the *Hamilton Princess* hotel (Pitt's Bay; phone: 295-3000); the *Southampton Princess* hotel (on Middle Rd. near Riddell's Bay; phone: 238-8000); and at the *Coral Beach Club* (phone: 236-2233).

Cécile Knitwear from all over the world, T-shirts, sweaters, dresses; lots of famous names, including Louis Feraud, Mondi, and Basler. Four locations: 15 Front St. (phone: 295-1311); the *Southampton Princess* hotel (on Middle Rd. near Riddell's Bay; phone: 238-1434); the *Sonesta Beach* hotel (Southampton; phone: 238-1924); and *Marriott's Castle Harbour* hotel (Tucker's Town; phone: 293-2841).

Crisson Real jewelry plus a good selection of Swiss watches. Locations on Queen St., Reid St., and two on Front St. (phone: 295-2351 for all); two branches in St. George's (York and Kent Sts.; phone: 297-0672; and Water St.; phone: 297-0107); also at *Marriott's Castle Harbour* hotel (Tucker's Town; phone: 293-2852); and the *Elbow Beach* hotel (Paget; phone: 236-9928).

Crown Colony Shop Women's fashions for day and evening from all over the world. 1 Front St. (phone: 295-3935), with a branch at *Somers Wharf,* St. George's (phone: 297-0311).

Davidson's of Bermuda Reasonably priced nautical garb and sportswear. Two Front St. stores, one opposite the ferry terminal (phone: 292-7137), and one near the West End (phone: 292-2080). Branches in the *Hamilton Princess* hotel (Pitt's Bay; phone: 292-2980); the *Southampton Princess* hotel (on Middle Rd. near Riddell's Bay; phone: 278-0105); *Marriott's Castle Harbour* hotel (Tucker's Town; phone: 293-2244); and Water St., St. George's (phone: 297-8363).

English Sports Shop A full line of fine clothing for men, women, and children from Europe, Great Britain, and the Far East. Cashmere, lamb's wool, and Shetland sweaters. Front St. (phone: 295-2672); branches at 14 locations including the *Hamilton Princess* hotel (Pitt's Bay; phone: 295-9691); the *Southampton Princess* hotel (on Middle Rd. near Riddell's Bay; phone: 238-1893); and the *Sonesta Beach* hotel (Southampton; phone: 238-8122).

E. R. Aubrey Gold and precious stone jewelry at prices as much as 35% below US prices. Front St. (phone: 295-3826).

Heritage House Truly beautiful and unusual, but not necessarily costly, gifts from all over the world. Brass, Perthshire paperweights, prints, original water-

colors and oils by Bermudian and international artists, and pewter m
tures are especially lovely. Also a selection of fine antiques. Front St. (p
295-2615). A branch, *The Admiral's Locker*, sells nautical gifts and unusual
Asian knickknacks. At the *Dockyard* (phone: 234-3835).

Irish Linen Shop Predictably stocked with good-looking placemats, tablecloths,
napkins, and the like; plus a fine selection of Madeira hand-embroidered
handkerchiefs. The only Bermuda outlet for Souleiado French Provençal
cottons, with totes, tops, and more to match. Also antique lace, and French
fabric by the yard at half what you'd pay in New York. Front St. (phone:
295-4089). There's also a branch on Cambridge Rd., Somerset (phone: 234-
0127).

Marks & Spencer The well-known British department store, offering high-quality
resortwear, sleepwear, and sweaters. Reid St. (phone: 295-0031).

Otto Wurz Lots of small treasures: charms, decanter labels, silver thimbles, coffee
spoons, English pewter mugs and flasks, and a bonanza of bangles. Front
St. (phone: 295-1257).

Pegasus Print and Map Shop Old prints, maps, framed and unframed; also hand-
colored miniatures framed in Bermuda cedar, an Andrew Wyeth print of
Ely's Harbour, and a large selection of greeting cards and ceramic house
signs. In an old Bermuda home on Pitt's Bay Rd., near the *Hamilton Princess*
hotel (phone: 295-2900).

The Perfume Shop The colony's largest collection of fine French perfumes at sub-
stantially discounted prices. The main store is on Front St. (phone: 295-
0570); a branch, called *The Guerlain Shop*, is on Queen St. (phone: 295-
5535 or 295-3755); another branch (also called *The Perfume Shop*) is on the
corner of King's Square and Water St., St. George's (phone: 297-1525).

Rubarb Fine needlepoint and tapestry designs, many with a Bermudian flavor.
Classes are offered. In a tiny cottage on Queen St., next to the library
(phone: 292-3336).

Sail On A unique shop selling exclusive lines of activewear from around the world,
the island's largest selection of T-shirts (voted best selection in Bermuda
by *Bermudian* magazine), and a colorful collection of unusual gifts. Old
Cellar La., off Front St. (phone: 295-0808).

Scottish Wool Shop Excellent buys on merino, Shetland, and lamb's wool sweaters,
and women's and children's kilts. Queen St. (phone: 295-0967).

Solomon's One-of-a-kind, hand-crafted jewelry made with unusual gems set in
18-karat gold and platinum. Front St. (phone: 292-4742 or 292-1003).

Triangles This small and exclusive boutique has the best prices anywhere on splashy
Diane Freis dresses. There are also designs by Adrienne Vittadini, and jewelry by Kai-Yin-Lo. Front St. (phone: 292-1990).

Vera P. Card Porcelain, figurines, china, crystal, precious jewelry, Hummel figurines, Bermuda's largest selection of clocks, Swiss watches including the Nivada quartz with a map of Bermuda on its face, Lladró Bermuda moongates, and Goebel longtails. Front St. West (phone: 295-1729) and Front St. East (phone: 292-0219). Branch stores at the *Sonesta Beach* hotel (Southampton; phone: 238-8122); *Marriott's Castle Harbour* hotel (Tucker's Town; phone: 293-2040); Water St., St. George's (phone: 297-1718); and York St., St. George's (phone: 297-1624).

Windjammer Gallery Original art, sculpture, limited-edition Bermuda prints, posters, and cards. In a traditional island cottage with a sculpture garden, on the corner of Reid and Kings Sts. (phone: 292-7861). A branch, called *The Print Pocket,* is located in the *Walker Arcade* off Front St. (phone: 295-8586).

Worth visiting elsewhere: *Taylors* (Water St., St. George's; phone: 297-1626), another good shop for sweaters; *Cow Polly East* (*Somers Wharf,* St. George's; phone: 297-1514), the place to find selected handicrafts and appealing gifts; and *Island Pottery* (phone: 234-3361) and the *Craft Market* (phone: 234-3208) at the *Dockyard. The Book Cellar* (Water St., St. George's; phone: 297-0448) has an excellent selection of books on Bermuda. *Victoriana* (*Clock Tower* building, *Dockyard;* phone: 234-1392) is a tiny shop filled with English antiques and Victorian memorabilia. *Rising Sun* (Middle Rd., Southampton; phone: 238-2154) has crafts, Bermudian culinary specialties, and interesting *Christmas* decorations.

SPORTS AND FITNESS

On land and sea, Bermuda's sports are of championship caliber all year long. Though most winter days are unsuitable for swimming, they're usually temperate and great for golf and tennis. In spring, summer, and fall, everyone plays everything.

AEROBICS Get a good workout at the *Sonesta Beach Spa* (at the *Sonesta Beach* hotel; phone: 238-1226), rated among the world's 10 best by "Lifestyles of the Rich and Famous." In Hamilton, try the *Athletic Club* (Washington St.; phone: 295-6140) or the *Olympic Club* (Dundonald St.; phone: 292-4095), each of which features a gym, a whirlpool, a sauna, and aerobics classes. Both are open to visitors for a fee.

BOATING Great Sound and Harrington Sound are the places, whether you skipper yourself or leave the pull-hauling to someone else and sign on for a sail on one of the several schooners that take groups out. Sunfish, roomier daysailers, and outboard motorboats can be rented; if you're in the mood for something bigger, skippered charters are offered aboard the 35-foot cruiser *Magic Carpet* (phone: 236-4863), which carries up to 18 people.

BEST IN BOATS

Bermuda is one of the world's sailing capitals; here are a few of our favorite charter companies.

Bermuda Caribbean Yacht Charter Capt. Hal White mans the *Night Wind,* a 52-foot ketch (phone: 238-8578 or 234-7266).

Longtail Cruises Capt. Neil Hansford-Smith sails *Longtail of Hinson's,* a 40-foot Cheoy Lee ketch (phone: 236-4482).

Mangrove Bay Marina Offers *Serenity,* a 40-foot Northstar ketch (phone: 234-0914 or 234-0331, ext. 295).

Ocean Yacht Charters Capts. Michael Smatt and Michael Voegeli sail two 41-foot craft, the *Water Gypsy* and *Ocean Spirit,* and the 51-foot *Spirit of the Wind* (phone: 234-8547 or 238-08250).

Sail Bermuda A team of Bermudian skippers sail *Alibi,* a 40-foot ketch, and *Sundancer,* a 50-foot Gulfstar ketch (phone: 238-0774).

Salt Kettle Boat Rentals Offers 41- and 55-foot sloops (phone: 236-4863 or 234-8165).

Sand Dollar Cruises Capt. Mark Whayman sails *Sand Dollar,* a 40-foot Bristol sloop (phone: 292-6104 or 234-8218).

Starlight Sailing Cruises Veteran Capt. Ed Williams sails his 31-foot sloop, *Starlight,* from Barr's Bay on Hamilton Harbour (phone: 292-1834).

Other rentals can be arranged at *Rance's Boatyard* (Crow La., Paget; phone: 292-1843); *Robinson's Charter Boat Marina* (at Somerset Bridge; phone: 234-0709 or 238-9408); *South Side Scuba* (at the *Grotto Bay Beach, Marriott's Castle Harbour,* and *Sonesta Beach* hotels; phone for all three: 293-2915); and *Bermuda Water Tours* (Hamilton; phone: 295-3727).

CRICKET This cousin of US baseball is played on pitches (fields) ranging from exquisitely manicured greens to vacant lots. Cricket is a spectator sport that is also a social event. The height of the cricket season in Bermuda is the *Cup Match Cricket Festival* (locals just call it the *Cup Match*) and *Somers Day*—usually the Thursday and Friday before the first Monday in August—when *St. George's* from the eastern end of the island meets *Somerset* from the western side. This is the only time Bermudians legally can gamble, and they enjoy a card game called "Crown & Anchor." For upcoming matches, consult the sports section of local newspapers.

GOLF Teeing up on any of the courses in Bermuda is one of life's consummate sporting joys, for all that advertising propaganda about swaying palms beside shimmering ponds is actually true on the golf courses of the island. But scenery aside, it is the superb tests of golf that prove the most powerful magnet to players who care only about challenging (and in some cases taming) the best. For most of us, just the experience of playing on one of the world's great courses is enough, and Bermuda offers plenty of extraordinary places that will satisfy even the most demanding golfer.

TOP TEE-OFF SPOTS

Belmont Challenging and undulating, this 18-hole, 5,777-yard course, designed by Scotsman Emmett Devereux, has been popular since its construction in 1923. Don't let the short scorecard distances lull you into a false sense of security; the trade winds make the listed lengths almost entirely superfluous.

The front nine is easier than the back nine, but the second hole's uphill challenge tests any player's mettle. The closed-in fairways make it difficult, too. Because of such hazards as a water hole and the double dogleg, many players have trouble reaching the par 5 number 11. The 14th is a long par 3, and Ian Crowe, director of golf, says: "If your game is really sour, the oldest Church of Scotland is open to all golfers, just across the street." Finishing uphill at number 18 is frustrating to many because the crystal caves beneath the surface sometimes cause the ball to roll unpredictably. Overlooking Hamilton Harbour in Warwick (phone: 236-1301).

Mid Ocean To find the consummate British golf atmosphere outside of Britain, you must come to Bermuda—and nowhere is the tradition of the Empire better maintained than on the links at *Mid Ocean.* Technically, it is a private club—and one that fiercely controls transient play—but we include it because there are ways in which a visitor usually can gain access to these otherwise exclusive premises. Most major hotels in Bermuda have at least one *Mid Ocean* member in their employ, and he or she is usually available to "introduce" hotel guests by contacting the club a day in advance. As a rule, Mondays, Wednesdays, and Fridays are the days on which such guests are made to feel at least marginally welcome, and golfers interested in challenging Bermuda's best may want to adjust their travel schedules accordingly.

The course is laid out in the finest linksland tradition, although the terrain is considerably more lush than most Scottish incarnations. There are carts available, a grudging recognition of the diminution in the number of available caddies. Still, walking these rolling hills, hopefully in the company of one of the surviving bag-toters who knows every knoll and roll, is best. The ultimate challenge here is the fabulous 5th hole, where a drive is forced to carry over a large lake and will find dry land only after a carry of about 200 yards. Even baseball's Babe Ruth was said to have had considerable trouble keeping out of the drink here, and chances are you will, too. And though the 5th is regularly included in the best 18 holes in the world, you may be hard-pressed to distinguish it from the 17 other *Mid Ocean* monsters that seem equally anxious to swallow your golf ball. Tucker's Town, St. George's (phone: 293-0330).

Port Royal Though lacking in *Mid Ocean's* exclusivity and cachet, *Port Royal* is still a worthy contender for the title of best in Bermuda. For some reason, public courses are generally denigrated in any links-by-links appraisal, and this is one case where such prejudice is really unfounded. Because of its rare (for Bermuda) watering system, *Port Royal* tends to stay in far better shape than *Mid Ocean* during Bermuda's hot, often arid summer, and there have been times when *Port Royal* has played deep and green while the other Bermuda courses presented fairways that were golden brown.

The 7th and 8th holes, a dogleg par 5 and windswept par 3 respectively, are the stars of the front nine, while the 16th hole, set on the craggy cliff (which is the nightmare of any player with vertigo), sets the tone for the home nine. If you're not afraid of heights, at least walk to the far championship tee on the 16th, though we'd be loath to suggest that you try to hit a ball from there. Some golfers we know have all but requested that a lifeline be secured to a nearby tree, lest they fall into the sea on their follow-through. It's quite a hole. Starting times can be reserved up to a year in advance. Middle Rd., Southampton (phone: 234-0974).

Riddell's Bay One of the island's most picturesque courses, and because it's laid out on a peninsula, you'll either be hitting balls over or playing parallel to Bermuda's azure waters. *Gibb's Hill Lighthouse* can be seen, too. The course was designed by Emmett Devereux; the clubhouse, which opened in 1922, is Bermuda's oldest. It's a nice walk around the 18 holes, but carts are also available. In order to play, an introduction by a member or your hotel management is required.

Challenges are faced in many places, but the first hole immediately separates the men from the boys. Its 427 yards form a formidable uphill par 4. The 8th hole (a par 4) is across 200 yards of water, but some players choose to go left and then right to avoid that challenge, turning it into a de facto par 5. There is no choice for the 9th hole, and making a strong shot across the water cannot be avoided. The 10th hole requires that you go up for a look at the green before hitting your second shot. Riddell's Bay, Southampton (phone: 238-1060 or 238-3225).

Other good greens include the hilltop *St. George's* course (phone: 297-8067 or 297-8148), redesigned by Robert Trent Jones Jr., and the course at *Marriott's Castle Harbour* (see *Checking In*). The *Southampton Princess* (phone: 238-0446) has a short, 18-hole "executive" (par 3) go-round; and there is a good public 9-hole course at the *Ocean View* hotel in Devonshire (phone: 236-6758).

HORSEBACK RIDING *Spicelands Riding Centre* (in Warwick; phone: 238-8246) offers breakfast rides and trail riding. *Lee Bow Riding Centre* (in Devonshire; phone: 236-4181) specializes in lessons for children.

JOGGING You'll spot joggers every day on every roadway (almost), but especially along the Railway Trail and on Tuesdays from early April to late October, when you can join the Bermudians for a 2-mile run that takes off at 6 PM from *Camden House* in the *Botanical Gardens.* For those in condition, there's also a 10-kilometer race and a marathon (26 miles) for international contestants every January.

SNORKELING AND SCUBA The beaches mentioned below, plus East and West Whale Bays on the South Shore, are best for snorkeling. The North Shore off Devonshire can be interesting, too. If your hostelry is on the beach, it probably will have fins, masks, and snorkels to lend or rent for a small fee; or you can buy gear in town—*International Sports Shop* (Bermudiana Rd., Hamilton; phone: 295-4183) carries a complete line.

Be aware that most shops will rent scuba equipment to and refill tanks for only those divers who have earned certification (through *YMCA* courses, which meet 1 or 2 nights a week for about 6 weeks, or through about a week of resort instruction, partly in a pool and partly in open water). For information, contact the *National Association of Underwater Instructors* (*NAUI;* PO Box 14650, 4650 Arrow Hwy., Suite F1, Montclair, CA 91763; phone: 714-621-5801); the *Professional Association of Diving Instructors* (*PADI;* 1251 E. Dyer Rd., Suite 100, Santa Ana, CA 92705; phone: 714-540-7234); or your local *YMCA.*

If you scuba dive or want to learn, *South Side Scuba* (see *Best in Boats,* above); *Blue Water Divers* (at Somerset Bridge; phone: 234-1034; fax: 234-3561); *Dive Bermuda* (at the *Dockyard;* phone: 234-0225; fax: 234-0723); *Fantasea* (near Hamilton in Pembroke; phone: 295-3052); and *Nautilus Diving* (at the *Southampton Princess;* phone: 238-2332; fax: 236-4284) are all set up to teach and to take you reef or wreck diving. And even if you can't dog-paddle, you can explore the Bermudian depths with *Greg Hartley's Under Sea Adventures* (phone: 234-2861) or *Hartley's Underwater Wonderland* (phone: 292-4434), which will provide you with a helmet straight out of Jules Verne and, after a few minutes' briefing, take you on a 3½ hour walk on the sea floor near Flatts Inlet.

SPECTATOR SPORTS On Sundays on fields all over the island, when Bermudians aren't playing, they're watching cricket from May through August, rugby and soccer from September through April. Sunday also means Sunfish racing on Harrington Sound, motorboat racing from May through October on Ferry Reach in St. George's, and go-cart racing year-round except July and August at the Naval Annex in Southampton. On Saturdays from March through October, top sailors race in the Great Sound. Check local newspapers for times and places.

SPORT FISHING One of the prime sport fishing grounds in the world, Bermuda attracts enthusiastic anglers from all over. Almost every variety of deepsea game fish, and many world-record-threatening catches, have been taken in these waters. Most of the fish seem to run during the spring-summer and summer-fall seasons, although there is no off-season on most islands—just better and poorer times to go out. Some of the fish run to deep waters, others lie among the reefs and shallows; but whatever style of fishing suits you—casting, trolling, bottom, or reef fishing—a challenge awaits in Bermuda.

Allison tuna, false albacore, wahoo, dolphin (the fish, not the mammal), oceanic bonito, blackfin tuna, rainbow runners, barracuda, and blue and white marlin are waiting in the deep. Horse-eye bonito, rockfish, yellowtail snapper, amberjack, and gray snapper are found in the reefs offshore. Bonefish and pompano are caught by shore anglers. Before taking a trip, ask in advance about the skipper's policy on caught fish; most captains will do their best to clean and fillet the day's catch for immediate consumption, or freeze and package it for direct shipment to the US.

The *Bermuda Charter Fishing Boat Association* (phone: 292-6246) can arrange a boat for you, as can the *Bermuda Sport Fishing Association* (phone: 295-2370) and the *St. George's Fishing and Cruising Association* (phone: 297-8093). Detailed information on independent charter fishing boats can be found in the *Bermuda Department of Tourism's Sports Guide;* or contact *Russell Young Fishing Co.* (in Somerset; phone: 234-1832) or Capt. Alan Card (also in Somerset; phone: 234-0872). Marinas rent rods and reels for shore fishing; or contact *Four Winds* fishing-tackle company (Woodlands Rd. on the outskirts of Hamilton; phone: 292-7466), which sells and rents equipment.

SWIMMING AND SUNNING Bermuda rightfully boasts some of the world's most beautiful beaches. It's true that—thanks to too many appearances on recurrent Most Beautiful lists—a few have been overdiscovered, but Horseshoe Bay remains gorgeous (and never too crowded) and Elbow Beach is still picture postcard—perfect (and fun). Many of the best beaches are found along Bermuda's dramatic southern coast; still others are tucked away in secluded coves on the north shore and the outer islands.

The pink sand on many of these beaches isn't an invention of the *Bermuda Department of Tourism*. It's quite real. The rosy specks among the white are actually weathered bits of red foram, a type of shell found among the offshore reefs. The white sand is made from calcium carbonate, the detritus of ancient shells and coral. Unlike ordinary beach sand, it is "soft," not gritty. Scientific explanations aside, take your shoes off and put it to the test.

DREAM BEACHES

The beaches below are not necessarily the *most* anything. They're simply nine of our favorites. Most of them are a bit off the beaten track; each has its particular charms. And they happen to be the ones of which we dream in the gray of mukluk season, when northern US city streets (and our spirits) are awash with slush and we desperately need emotional uplifting.

Astwood Cove An idyllic spot for swimming, sunning, and picnicking, it's a steep climb down from South Road, away from 20th-century disturbances. This is still one of the island's lesser-known treasures; please *don't* spread the word. Warwick Parish.

Church Bay The descent to this secluded stretch offers the best views of the turquoise and green bay and the reefs that punctuate it. Although the beach itself is small, there's plenty of pink sand, and swimming here is spectacular. Scuba diving and snorkeling are excellent, too. There are restrooms at the top of the hill, near the parking area. Southampton Parish.

Elbow Beach There's easy access from South Road via Tribe Road No. 4 to one of Bermuda's top sun and swim spots. The beach stretches for about a mile from the western end past the private *Coral Beach Club* to the east at the *Elbow Beach* hotel. A lunch wagon is here daily during the spring and summer. Wear a bathing suit under your clothing; there are no changing facilities. Paget Parish.

Horseshoe Bay One of the most popular—and most often photographed–beaches on the island, it's a great place to swim—and even better, to walk. Explore the hills and the cave-like formations at the western end before you take the plunge into its turquoise waters. Snack bar and changing rooms are on site. Southampton Parish.

John Smith's Bay A short stroll from Devil's Hole Hill leads to this small swath of beach on the south coast. This is a perfect place for a picnic. Offshore, there's good snorkeling and scuba diving. Restrooms and changing facilities are on site. Smith's Parish.

Natural Arches Towering above the beach at the private *Mid Ocean Club,* these coral and limestone formations provide a dramatic backdrop to this stretch of sand along Bermuda's southern coast. Although the club is private, the beach—where the sand is pinker than almost anywhere on the island—is open to the public. Tucker's Town, St. George's Parish.

Somerset Long Bay This sandy stretch near the island's western end is an ideal place to watch the sun go down. Part of the *Long Bay Nature Reserve,* it's also a great spot for bird watching. Like the mood that prevails here, the waters are calm—good for children and adults who aren't strong swimmers. The beach has restrooms and changing facilities. Sandys Parish.

Spanish Point Park Composed of a series of little coves and beaches, this is a good place to drop anchor and enjoy a swim. If you haven't brought a picnic basket, there's usually a lunch wagon here from spring through early fall. There are also restrooms. Pembroke Parish.

Warwick Long Bay It *is* long and soft and truly pink and—compared to famous Horseshoe Bay, just down the coast—utterly serene from sunup to sunset, perfect for private picnicking, lazy sunning, and sand castle sculpting. Bermudians love it and neighboring Jobson's Cove and Stonehole and Chaplin Bays for late afternoon dips. There are restrooms at the western end. Just off South Rd. in Warwick Parish.

Most inland and town hotels have beach club affiliations or provide beach transport for their guests, but more adventurous visitors bike out, taking picnics from their hotels. Officially, Bermudians swim from *Bermuda Day* (May 24) till *Labour Day* (the first Monday in September) only. Visitors aren't that limited–any warm day any time of year will do. Though you can't count on specific dates, there are almost always some good beach days in December, January, and February. In addition to the beaches, most hotels and guesthouses have pools—some indoors.

TENNIS Bermuda is the undisputed tennis capital of the Atlantic and has been since the game was imported here from England in 1873 (the first court to be laid out in the western Atlantic was at Clermont in Paget Parish). Today, there are 85 courts throughout the island—some at hotels, some public, some attached to clubs that allow non-members to play for a fee—that are fine for an occasional game. Serious players—and those who want to get serious—will find their search limited to those resorts with resident pros, an ample number of courts, programs of lessons, and lights for night play. Since the game is so popular, it's always a good idea to reserve a day ahead whenever possible.

CHOICE COURTS

Coral Beach A very exclusive private club, but chances are you can play, too. Introduction by a member is required for entrance. Facilities include 8 Har-Tru courts (2 lighted) and a pro shop. Tennis whites are mandatory. Derek Singleton is the head pro; lessons are available. Every year the *Bermuda Lawn Tennis Club Invitational* and the *Coral Beach Invitational* tournaments are held here. Paget (phone: 236-2233 or 236-6495).

Elbow Beach There are 5 Laykold courts, 2 lighted. Lessons are available from pro Eugene Woods. Tennis packages are offered. Paget (phone: 236-3535).

Government Tennis Stadium Thoroughly public facilities with 6 clay courts (2 asphalt, 3 lighted), a pro shop, and a ball machine. Private lessons with teaching pro Eugene Woods are available. Tennis attire is mandatory. Cedar Ave. north of Hamilton (phone: 292-0105).

Grotto Bay Beach Facilities include 4 Plexipave courts; 2 are available for night play. Pro Ray Knight gives lessons; video analysis is available on request. Tennis packages are offered. Hamilton Parish (phone: 293-8333).

Marriott's Castle Harbour This hotel has 6 hard courts; pro Eddie Kyme gives lessons. Tucker's Town; St. George's (phone: 293-2040).

Southampton Princess The island's top tennis resort, with excellent programs for adults and children. There are 11 Plexipave courts (3 lighted). Director of tennis is Bruce Sims; Debbie Harper is the pro. Southampton (phone: 238-1005).

Another good tennis venue is the *Port Royal Club* (Middle Rd., Southampton; phone: 234-0974), which offers 4 Plexipave courts in a beautiful setting. Many hotels offer tennis packages with guaranteed court time built in, which make great sense if you're keen on the game. Check with your travel agent. Squash addicts can set up playing time with a call to the *Bermuda Squash Racquets Club* (in Devonshire; phone: 292-6881).

WATER SKIING The protected waters of the Great Sound, Castle Harbour, and Mangrove Bay are best for water skiing. *Bermuda Waterski Centre* (phone: 234-3354) and *Bermuda Water Skiing* (phone: 293-3328 or 293-3333, ext. 37) rent boats; lessons are also available.

WINDSURFING *Mangrove Marina* (Cambridge Rd., Somerset; phone: 234-0914 or 234-0331, ext. 295) and *South Side Scuba* (see *Best in Boats,* above) give windsurfing lessons. Equipment rentals are available from *South Side Scuba.*

NIGHTCLUBS AND NIGHTLIFE

For a place that has never claimed to have much to do after dark, Bermuda actually has a good deal. No Las Vegas–style nudie shows or chorus lines, and early golf tomorrow may mean a 10 o'clock bedtime tonight. But there's considerable action when you're in the mood. Far and away the prettiest places for cocktails and sunset watching are the *Gazebo Lounge* of the *Hamilton Princess* hotel (see *Checking In*) from which you can watch the lights blink on all around the harbor and beyond; the terrace of the *Palm Reef* hotel (Harbour Rd., Paget; phone: 236-1000), with its view of Hamilton bathed in an incredible peach-colored light (you really have to be there); and the dramatically situated terrace or poolside of the *Reefs* hotel (see *Checking In*) overlooking its own South Shore beach. After dinner, the big hotels schedule different shows each night; the *Talbot Brothers,* Gene Steede, and *Hubert Smith and the Coral Islanders* continue to be long-run favorites, and there are the usual limbo and calypso bands and combos to fill in. Smaller hotels and guesthouses do more intimate numbers—often with a calypso singer or a solo piano supplying dinner music. The *Clay House Inn* (North Shore Rd., Devonshire; phone: 292-3193 or 293-9265) puts on the liveliest island show around—lots of limbo, calypso, steel band music, and dancing; best call ahead for reservations. The *Clay House* also plays host to occasional traveling musicals from the States. Liveliest stops on the pub circuit are *Rum Runners* (Front St., Hamilton; phone: 292-4737); *Ye Olde Cock and Feather* (Front St., Hamilton; phone: 295-2263); *Robin Hood* (Richmond Rd., Hamilton; phone: 295-3314); and *Spazzizi's* at the *Elbow Beach* hotel (see *Checking In*). A low-key alternative is the friendly, intimate bar at the *Show Bizz* restaurant (see *Eating Out*).

But the really big move in Bermuda is in the disco direction. The under-40 crowd heads for *Oasis* (in the Emporium Building, Front St., Hamilton; phone: 292-4978), where *karaoke* singing makes every person a star. Popular with Bermuda's yuppie crowd, *Oscar's* (below the *Monte Carlo* restaurant on Victoria St., Hamilton; phone: 292-0348) has a Bermuda cottage–style bar and a cedar-paved dance floor. *The Club* (above *Little Venice* on Bermudiana Rd., Hamilton; phone: 295-6693) is the current favorite of the over-30, tie-and-jacket smart set; the cover charge is waived if you have dinner at the *Harbourfront* (Front St., Hamilton; phone: 295-4207), *Little Venice,* or *La Trattoria* restaurants (see *Eating Out* for the latter two). The *Bayview Lounge* at *Marriott's Castle Harbour* (see *Checking In*) has a trio of instrumentalists most nights, and the hotel's *Blossoms Lounge* features a live band, harking back to a gentler touch-dancing era. Out at the *Dockyard, Club 21* (phone: 234-2721) offers American jazz and pop artists such as Richie Havens. For the more adventurous, in Hamilton's "back of town" (the area behind Front Street) is *Hubie's* (Angle St.; phone: 293-9287; open until 10 PM), a lively neighborhood jazz club where on any given night, you could meet anyone from a local fisherman to a Swedish tourist to one of Bermuda's leading politicians.

Best on the Island

CHECKING IN

Bermuda probably has more attractive guestrooms per square mile than any other resort island in the world. Basically, its accommodations fall into four different categories: hotels, cottage colonies, housekeeping apartments and cottages, and guesthouses. For information on rental options and accommodations discounts, see GETTING READY TO GO.

For the purposes of this guide, $270 or more a night (in season) for two people with breakfasts and dinners (MAP) is considered expensive; $150 to $270 a night for two (MAP) is considered moderate; $150 and below for two (MAP) is considered inexpensive. Some hotels also offer EP rates (without meals); others offer CP (with continental breakfast) or BP (with full Bermudian breakfast). Rates without meals run $35 to $45 per person per night below MAP rates. Unless otherwise stated, all hotels listed below are air conditioned and feature private baths. In recent years, more and more hotels on Bermuda are refusing to accept credit cards (even some of the more expensive places); it's a good idea to check when making your reservation. The cottage colonies often will not take credit cards, either, but they will honor personal checks with advance notice. Here, too, double-check the payment policy in advance. Mid-November through March prices can mean savings of up to 40% on airfare and accommodations packages. If you're planning a winter holiday, note that a number of hotels close for periods as short as 2 weeks or as long as 2 months sometime between December 1 and March 1. All telephone numbers are in the 809 area code unless otherwise indicated.

For an unforgettable island experience, we begin with our favorites (pricey, but worth it), followed by our recommendations of cost and quality choices of resort hotels, small hotels, cottage colonies, housekeeping cottages and apartments, and guesthouses—listed by price category.

SPECIAL HAVENS

Cambridge Beaches The ultimate getaway without the glitz, this lovely pink-and-white paradise sits on terraced hillsides at the westernmost tip of Bermuda. Most of the 82 cottages overlook the Atlantic, and if serenity is the thing for which you long, try breakfast on your patio with nothing between you and the rest of the world but an incredibly blue ocean and an occasional longtail. Seventy-plus and still going strong, Bermuda's grande dame has a loyal following—plaques in the main house bear the names of guests who have visited here more than 60 times! For those who seek activity, there's a saltwater pool, 3 tennis courts (afternoon tea is held at the covered spectators' area on mixed doubles days), an 8,000-

square-foot putting green (the *Port Royal* golf course is nearby), a croquet lawn, a marina equipped with an impressive group of sail-, motor-, and rowboats (with glass-bottom boat excursions also available), and shuttle service to Hamilton for shoppers. This property's latest addition, a fully equipped European spa, rounds out the amenities. Dinner is a delightfully formal affair, made even more memorable thanks to the creative talents of chef Jean-Claude Garzia and a staff that makes you feel their only mission in life is to please you (see *Eating Out*); there's also entertainment (thankfully, no disco!) nightly. If you think all this sounds like heaven—it is. Somerset (phone: 234-0331; 800-468-7300; fax: 234-3352).

Horizons Set on a hillside overlooking Bermuda's southern coast, this member of the prestigious Relais & Châteaux group is one of the prettiest properties on the island. Elegantly appointed, private guest cottages—with evocative names such as "Banana Tree" and "Sea Cloud"—dot the verdant landscape; many of the 48 rooms in the cottages and the main house boast ocean views (the "Roundelay" cottage is our favorite). Guests can enjoy a game of tennis on one of 3 Har-Tru tennis courts, a round of golf on the 9-hole course, practice on the 18-hole putting green, or a swim in the pool; then relax over lunch at a poolside terrace, enjoy cocktails in one of the spacious lounges in the main house, and dine in more formal surroundings on continental dishes prepared by a staff of internationally trained chefs. Afternoon tea is served daily, and there are weekly swizzle parties, barbecues, and buffet suppers. For beach-loving guests, there is access to the exclusive *Coral Beach Club* just across the road. Paget (phone: 236-0048; 800-468-0022; fax: 236-1981).

Lantana Colony Club Nestled along terraced hillsides in serene Sandys Parish, this exclusive complex of cottages and waterfront suites affords a welcome respite from the hectic workaday world. Guests can do as much—or as little–as they choose on this 20-acre property that includes 64 suites distributed among several charming cottages, a private beach, a pool, 2 Har-Tru tennis courts, a putting green, 2 croquet lawns, shuffleboard, bike rental, and a private dock that offers water skiing and rents Sunfish. For golfers, the *Port Royal* course is nearby. For cocktails, there's an ocean-view patio or the informal *Meridian Lounge*. And when the sun sets, the flower-decked solarium dining room offers a fine continental menu (see *Eating Out*). No wonder this place draws repeat visitors. Somerset Bridge, Somerset (phone: 234-0141; 800-468-3733; fax: 234-2562).

Newstead Situated on a hillside overlooking Hamilton Harbour and the busy capital city, this establishment's well-groomed gardens and tranquil terraces offer perfect vantage points for watching the maneuvers of the huge cruise ships and freighters that dock in the harbor. And going to Hamilton is easy—all you have to do is walk down the steps to the ferry landing. There are 54 charming rooms (ask for one with a harbor view) spread among the original manor house and cottage suites. The stately main house offers all the comforts and a house party atmosphere—large living room with fireplace, library, cozy bar with horse and fox hunting prints, and an elegant dining room. Deep-water swimming in the harbor can be enjoyed from the hotel's private dock, or you can take a dip in the heated pool, relax on the sun patio, and enjoy a sauna. Beach privileges are also available at the *Coral Beach Club*. *'Brellas,* the terrace restaurant, is a pleasant setting for a light snack or a sandwich (see *Eating Out*). Sailboat rentals are available from the dock, and 2 Har-Tru tennis courts, a putting green, and a gameroom are on the property. Evening entertainment—calypso music and a harpist—and delicious barbecue dinners and swizzle parties round out the intimate, private residence atmosphere. Harbour Rd., Paget (phone: 236-6060; 800-468-4111; fax: 236-7454).

Reefs The dramatic blue and turquoise of the Atlantic and a broad swath of private beach are the focal points of this cliffside cottage colony. You'll hear the constant soothing sounds of waves rolling onto the beach at Christian Bay—a world away from the familiar. This is a well-run establishment, a fact attested to by the number of repeat visitors. Its 65 tastefully furnished lanai and cabaña rooms, plus cottages, sit on terraced tiers overlooking the beach and the ocean. Swimming is as you like it: in the crystal-clear Atlantic or the heated pool. There's *Coconuts*—a fine restaurant and beach bar (see *Eating Out*)–and another more formal dining room, as well as lounges and terraces for cocktails. Good entertainment—calypso, piano, or dancing—is a regular feature, and every week there's a swizzle party, buffet, and barbecue. Snorkeling (there is an abundance of colorful fish in these waters) is right off the beach; good scuba diving sights are nearby. Other facilities include 2 tennis courts, a fitness center with exercise room, and a shuffleboard court in a garden setting. South Shore, Southampton (phone: 238-0222; 800-223-1363; fax: 238-8372).

Southampton Princess Far and away Bermuda's largest, this 600-room hotel holds court on a hilltop overlooking the sea, and it seems that the view stretches all the way to England. Maintaining a personalized touch despite its size, this property does its regal name proud. Room service is prompt—and the coffee is hot; a massage at the spa is worth a king's ransom; and the executive golf course is great fun to play. You can stroll the grounds and then head across the road to the hotel's own sheltered beach, hop a ferry into town, or just people watch in the bustling lobby. Aside from golf, facilities include tennis courts, a shopping arcade (with branches of some of Hamilton's main shops), and indoor and outdoor pools. When you get hungry, you can choose from among 6 hotel eateries (we recommend the *Waterlot,* see *Eating Out* for details). Southampton (phone: 238-8000; 800-223-1818; fax: 238-8968).

RESORT HOTELS

EXPENSIVE

Belmont On 114 acres, this 151-room Forte resort boasts its own 18-hole golf course, complete with clubhouse and resident pro; a 9-hole, 95-yard, flood-lit miniature golf course; 3 lighted, all-weather tennis courts; and plenty of space for strolling. Guests also can take advantage of the free transportation to Horseshoe Bay Beach, and a dock for the ferry to Hamilton is directly adjacent. Entertainment, several dining rooms, and an inviting bar round out the facilities. Outdoor barbecue parties are held weekly from May to October. Overlooking Hamilton Harbour in Warwick (phone: 236-1301; 800-225-5843; fax: 236-6867).

Elbow Beach Overlooking this 50-acre resort's long pink beach are 295 elegant suites and guestrooms in all kinds of permutations: balconied bedrooms, duplex cottages, lanai rooms overlooking pool and ocean, and surfside lanais. All rooms feature silk-draped walls and marble baths. There is good tennis on 4 courts, a pool on a hillside, a beach with terraces, a snack bar, the popular *Café Lido,* a gameroom, and a small health club with exercise machines. Dancing and shows are offered most nights. Paget (phone: 236-3535; 800-822-4200; fax: 236-8043).

Grotto Bay Beach The setting of this 21-acre oceanfront property is serene, despite the fact that it's only minutes from the airport. There are 201 rooms with private balconies and wide sea views; a small beach; a pool; 2 bars; boating; a full scuba program; 4 tennis courts; and unique caves on the property, site of daily grotto swims. The inviting poolside *Moongate Terrace* restaurant holds barbecues and parties. There's also an excellent children's program. At the edge of Hamilton Parish (phone: 293-8333; 800-582-3190; fax: 293-2306).

Hamilton Princess At the edge of Hamilton Harbour, it's classy and classic, with extremely pleasant service. There are 447 rooms, many with balconies; 2 oceanside pools; 3 restaurants; shopping arcades; a beauty salon; and a health club with exercise machines and sauna. Transportation is provided to the *Southampton Princess* beach club, tennis courts, and 18-hole "executive" golf course, with which the hotel has complete exchange privileges. Shows are staged nightly from April through October. Pitt's Bay (phone: 295-3000; 800-223-1818; fax: 295-1914).

Harmony Club The island's only all-inclusive resort—rates at this 78-room club include accommodations, meals, drinks, taxes, tips, moped rental, and admission to the nearby *Oasis* nightclub in Hamilton. Lush gardens—carefully planted throughout the year—add a perennially colorful backdrop. There are 2 tennis courts, a putting green, a pool, 2 saunas, and a whirlpool. On South Rd. in Paget, just 5 minutes from Hamilton by taxi or moped and on the main bus route (phone: 236-3500; 800-225-5843; fax: 236-2624).

Marriott's Castle Harbour A completely self-contained resort, it's set on a historic 250-acre property overlooking Castle Harbour (where else?). In addition to 402 rooms and attractive, airy common areas, the resort includes 3 pools, 3 restaurants (*Mikado's,* serving first-rate Japanese cuisine; *Windsor,* continental; and the *Golf Grill*), a shopping arcade, a health club with Jacuzzi, full convention facilities (which are usually too filled with conventioneers for most individual vacationers), tennis courts, beaches on the property offering full water sports, beautifully manicured grounds, and a free shuttle to a nearby off-premises beach. The championship golf course is one of Bermuda's best (see *Golf*). Tucker's Town (phone: 293-2040; 800-228-9290; fax: 293-8288).

Sonesta Beach On two of its own South Shore beaches, this resort is in splendid shape following a recent $15-million renovation. Its 401 guestrooms include 26 split-level suites; all have balconies overlooking the sea or the adjacent sheltered bays. The property has 2 heated pools (1 bubble-roofed), a garden patio, and a shopping arcade. A handsome, expertly run European/American spa and health club is a big plus. Dinner and dancing (the cheek-to-cheek variety) are offered nightly in the 2-tiered dining room of *Lillian's* restaurant, and there's a comedy show nightly except Sundays. Southampton (phone: 238-8122; 800-SONESTA; fax: 238-8463).

SMALL HOTELS

EXPENSIVE

Pompano The small, inviting central clubhouse here is surrounded by a pretty colony of 52 one-bedroom suites and deluxe rooms overlooking the South Shore sea. There's a hillside pool, a beach, a water sports center (open May through October), and 2 oceanside Jacuzzis; scuba diving is easily arranged. Other features include a cozy bar, a lounge, a dining room with a view, and nightly entertainment. The property adjoins the *Port Royal* golf course; 4 tennis courts also are available at *Port Royal*. Middle Rd., Southampton (phone: 234-0222; 508-358-2612 in Massachusetts; 800-343-4155 elsewhere in the US; fax: 234-1694).

Stonington Beach This place is special because its very professional top management heads a staff made up almost entirely of students enrolled in *Bermuda College*'s Hotel Technology Department; resulting student-supervisor teamwork means double service for guests. The property consists of a good-looking Bermuda-modern main building, plus several 2-story, 16-room units built into the hills above a small, idyllic South Shore beach. There are attractive public spaces, especially a cozy library with a fireplace, and 64 less attractive double rooms, but all have ocean views and terraces. Highlight include formal dining in the *Norwood Room,* a pool, an exquisite beach adjacent to the hotel, beach privileges at the *Elbow Beach* hotel, 2 tennis courts, and afternoon tea in the lobby and adjoining lounges. Bermuda Beach Rd., Paget (phone: 236-5416; 800-447-7462; fax: 236-0371).

Waterloo House This elegant, small-scale harborside hostelry is a member of the Relais & Châteaux group; staying here is a lot like being at the house party of a well-to-do British/Bermudian family. All 31 rooms feature bright decor warmed with antiques. There are wonderful views, and Hamilton is just a 3-minute walk away. In addition to the main house, there are 5 lodges, a pleasant restaurant, a bar, a dining terrace (the gasoline fumes emanating from the dockside filling station are sometimes a definite negative here), and a pool. On the outskirts of Hamilton (phone: 295-4480; 800-468-4100; fax: 295-2585).

MODERATE

Palmetto A pleasant place on Harrington Sound and handy to all the water sports thereon. White-roofed in the Bermuda tradition, it has 40 rooms and cottages, all with balconies or terraces; a lovely parlor; pretty gardens; a pool; a small beach; free transportation to other beaches; and the chummy *Ha'Penny Pub* (with a super bar and an extra-super bartender), a favored drop-in spot at lunchtime and after dinner. The hotel's *Inlet* restaurant is pleasing and popular, too (see *Eating Out*). Flatts Village, Smith's (phone: 293-2323; 800-982-0026; fax: 293-8761).

Rosedon This property has 43 rooms (one an inexpensive single) in and around a colonial house surrounded by well-maintained lawns and gardens. There's a large, heated pool, and tennis and beach privileges are available at the nearby *Elbow Beach* hotel (free transportation is provided). Breakfast is complimentary, and other meals are provided upon request (there is no dining room). Within walking distance of shops, ferry, and restaurants. Paget (phone: 295-1640; 800-225-5567; fax: 295-5904).

COTTAGE COLONIES

EXPENSIVE

Ariel Sands The atmosphere is relaxed at this South Shore property, which has 48 rooms in cottages by the ocean, a private beach, freshwater and saltwater pools, 3 tennis courts (2 of which are lighted), a patio, an attractive restaurant, and an inviting bar. Devonshire (phone: 236-1010; 800-468-6610; fax: 236-0087).

Fourways No longer just a fine restaurant (be sure to see *Eating Out*), it has expanded to include 5 luxury cottages of 2 units each (all with private balconies, patios, well-equipped bathrooms, and kitchenettes), a pool, and pretty gardens. The feeling is very much akin to being an island resident. Close to the beach and 10 minutes from Hamilton, on Middle Rd. (phone: 236-6517; 800-962-7654; fax: 236-5528).

Pink Beach On a private South Shore beach, it has 81 rooms in cottages rambling over a seaside estate. The prestigious *Mid Ocean Club* is 5 minutes away, handy for avid golfers. A large pool, a sun terrace, and fine tennis are other pluses. The toaster in your room is used by the room service waiter/waitress each morning (God forbid the toast should be cold!) after breakfast has been set on the patio. There's no restaurant. Smith's (phone: 293-1666; 203-655-4200 in Connecticut; 800-422-1323 elsewhere in the US; fax: 293-8935).

St. George's Club It's sometimes difficult to get one of the 69 rental units in this first class time-share property perched on a hill overlooking St. George's. There are fully equipped, pretty cottages, a dining room, a pub, a lounge, 3 pools (one heated in cooler months), and tennis. Guests pay reduced fees at the *St. George's* golf course next door. Off York St., with an entrance on Rose Hill off the main road into St. George's (phone: 297-1200; fax: 297-8003).

HOUSEKEEPING COTTAGES AND APARTMENTS

MODERATE

Clear View Set at the water's edge between Hamilton and St. George's, it has 27 rooms in 7 comfortable cottages, 2 pools, a tennis court, and an art gallery; painting and drawing lessons are available from an artist-in-residence. There's no restaurant. Sandy La., Hamilton (phone: 293-2067; 800-468-9600; fax: 293-0267).

Garden House On the road to Somerset, this small 3-acre property offers 2 secluded self-contained studios and a cottage. There's a pool, but no restaurant; harbor swimming is possible nearby. Middle Rd., Somerset Bridge (phone: 234-1435; fax: 234-3006).

Grape Bay Nestled among bay grape arbors, overlooking a beautiful beach, this place is also close to the bustling city of Hamilton. Both of the 2-bedroom cottages have fireplaces and fully equipped kitchens. There's no restaurant. South Rd., Paget (phone: 236-1194; 800-637-4116; fax: 236-1662).

Longtail Cliffs Perfect for families, here are 13 units (mostly 2-bedroom, 2-bath, some with fireplaces) with TV sets, and terraces that overlook the Atlantic.

There's no restaurant. South Rd., Warwick. For information, write PO Box HM 836, Hamilton HMCX, Bermuda (phone: 236-2822; 800-637-4116; fax: 236-5178).

Marley Beach Cottages Spectacularly perched above its own South Shore beach, this pretty offers stunning views from the heated freshwater pool. There are 13 apartments, some with fireplaces. It's secluded, but handy to restaurants (there are none on the property) and nightlife; Hamilton, golf, and tennis are a short bus ride away. South Rd., Warwick (phone: 236-1143; 800-637-4116; fax: 236-1984).

Munro Beach Overlooking the sea beside *Port Royal*'s scenic 16th hole, this friendly, family-run place is perfect for golf and tennis buffs. Families like it, too. There are 16 cottage apartments; no restaurant or pool, but a pleasant, secluded, private beach. Southampton (phone: 234-1175; fax: 234-3528).

Surf Side Beach Club Secluded, and overlooking its own very nice South Shore beach, this varied group of 37 apartments and cottage units is decorated in good-looking Bermuda-contemporary style. The atmosphere is extremely pleasant; the buildings and grounds, well maintained. There's a coffee shop. Warwick (phone: 236-7100; 800-553-9990; fax: 236-9765).

INEXPENSIVE

Angel's Grotto With 7 apartments on Harrington Sound (ask for a water view), this property offers a nice sense of privacy, yet it's within easy reach of Flatts Village, water sports, beaches, restaurants, and sites to see. Mrs. Hart is the thoughtful resident owner. There's no restaurant. Hamilton Parish (phone: 293-1986; 800-637-4116; fax: 292-1243).

Astwood Cove A small, shining white complex of 8 suites and 12 studio apartments, each with neat kitchenette and a patio or balcony overlooking both the pool and the South Shore ocean vista through the trees across the way. On-site amenities include a sauna, a small pool, laundry facilities, and gas-fired barbecues; guests may pick fruit from the property's citrus and banana trees. There's no restaurant. South Rd., Warwick (phone: 236-0984; 800-441-7087; fax: 236-1164).

Pretty Penny This little property is large on old-fashioned charm. It offers 7 studio apartments with kitchen facilities, a small garden pool, and privacy (but no restaurant). For the most secluded quarters, ask for the separate "Play Penny" cottage. Cobb's Hill Rd., Paget (phone: 236-1194; 800-637-4116; fax: 236-1662).

Whale Bay Inn Overlooking *Port Royal* golf course and Whale Bay Beach, this family-run operation has 5 units with TV sets and radios (but no restaurant). It's private, yet convenient to the bus, supermarket, beach, and restaurants. Southampton (phone: 238-0469; 800-637-4116; fax: 238-1224).

GUESTHOUSES

MODERATE

Oxford House Convenient to shopping and restaurants in downtown Hamilton, this elegantly furnished 12-room guesthouse (the closest to Hamilton) offers complimentary full buffet breakfast with freshly baked goodies everyday (there's no restaurant on the premises). The rooms have TV sets and telephones. For information, write PO Box 374, Hamilton HMBX, Bermuda (phone: 295-0503; 800-548-7758; fax: 295-0250).

Royal Heights This small, pleasantly managed, modern spot has a stunning view of *Riddell's Bay* golf course and the sounds (Great and Little) from a Southampton hillside. There are 6 spacious guestrooms, some with terraces and kitchenettes, a small pool, and lovely common rooms, but no restaurant. On Lighthouse Hill, near the *Southampton Princess* (phone: 238-0043; fax: 238-8445).

INEXPENSIVE

Hillcrest Tucked away in the historic, sleepy lanes of St. George's, this attractive former sea captain's house with 10 comfortable (if plain) rooms is convenient to the Olde Towne's many shops and restaurants (there's no restaurant on the premises). Proprietor E. Trew Robinson offers Old World hospitality to blend with the surroundings. Nea's Alley, St. George's (phone: 297-1630).

Little Pomander On a quiet residential street just 5 minutes from Hamilton and overlooking Hamilton Harbour's eastern end, here are 2 tastefully decorated cottages housing 9 guestrooms, 3 of which have kitchenettes. Patio and barbecue facilities are available (but there's no restaurant). 16 Pomander Rd., Paget (phone: 236-7635; 800-637-4116; fax: 236-8332).

Pleasant View In Princess Estate, a quiet section of Pembroke Parish, this family home with a sweeping North Shore view offers 4 double rooms, 1 studio, and 1 apartment suitable for a family of four. All are pin neat and nicely cared for by a pleasant couple. There is a pool on the premises, but no restaurant (phone: 292-4520).

Royal Palms Within walking distance of Hamilton, this recently renovated, Edwardian-style, former private residence retains its turn-of-the-century charm . There are 8 rooms in the main house and 2 rooms and 1 apartment in adjoining cottages, all in a pleasant garden setting. A pool and the popular *Ascot's* restaurant are also here. 24 Rosemont Ave., Pembroke (phone: 292-1854; 800-637-4116; fax: 292-1946).

Salt Kettle House On the water west of Hamilton, it has 4 cottages and 4 rooms, some with kitchens. Rates include breakfast; there's no restaurant, however. 10 Salt Kettle Rd., Paget (phone: 236-0407; fax: 236-8639).

EATING OUT

Bermudian food is surprisingly good these days, although most meat still has to be imported. Knowledgeable diners stick to the wide (and excellent) variety of seafood; specialties include tangy mussel pie, Bermuda fish chowder liberally laced with sherry peppers and black rum, sweet Bermuda lobster (in season, September through March), large tiger shrimp that look a lot like rock lobsters (called guinea chicks), and traditional Hoppin' John (black-eyed peas and rice). At *Christmastime,* visitors will also be treated to cassava pie—no Bermudian *Yule* would be complete without it. An item called Bermuda fish is found on most menus without additional reference. It will be whatever's been caught that day, and is served either pan-fried or broiled. Try it. If you're invited to a "Bermuda Breakfast," expect to find codfish, potatoes, and various condiments.

A number of British-accented pubs are fun for lunch, an informal supper, and/or a sociable pint or two before or after dinner. At one of these establishments, dinner for two can cost as little as $25 to $35, plus drinks and tip. From November to March, many fine restaurants participate in a "dine-around" program, serving full-course meals at slightly reduced prices. *Stonington Beach, Cambridge Beaches, Lantana Colony Club,* and the *Reefs* offer their guests carousel dining year-round. Most of the major restaurants request that men wear jackets for dinner, and a number require both jacket and tie; however, the trend in recent years is toward more casual dress on some nights. When in doubt, check. Neat but casual clothes are okay for Bermuda's favorite meal, Sunday brunch, which is more apt to feature a big buffet than crêpes and eggs Benedict; it's especially good at the *Elbow Beach* hotel, *Fourways, Henry VIII,* and the *Waterlot* (our favorite because of the good Dixieland jazz—also see *Quintessential Bermuda* in DIVERSIONS). For dinner (including a cocktail and service charge) at restaurants listed as expensive, expect to pay more than $100 per couple; moderate, $60 to $100; inexpensive, less than $60. All telephone numbers are in the 809 area code unless otherwise indicated.

ST. GEORGE'S

EXPENSIVE

Carriage House Lantern-lit and romantic at night, this place features shrimp dishes, prime beef, and a salad bar for both lunch and dinner. Children's dishes also are available. The Sunday champagne brunch is something special, so is afternoon tea. The service is pleasant (though sometimes slow). Closed *Christmas* and *New Year's Day.* Reservations advised. Major credit cards accepted. Water St. at *Somers Wharf* (phone: 297-1270 or 297-1730).

MODERATE

Black Horse Tavern A friendly, informal outpost, it purveys such home-cooked local fare as fine Bermuda chowder, conch stew, pan-fried fish steaks, stuffed rock lobster, and other fresh seafood. This is the place to hobnob with locals, and to gaze out at Smith's and Paget Islands. Closed Mondays and *Christmas*. No reservations. Major credit cards accepted. On St. David's Island (phone: 293-9724).

O'Malley's Pub on the Square Housed in a historic building dating from 1785, it still has its original cedar-beamed ceiling. Typical pub food, plus Bermuda fish dishes, are served. Open daily. Reservations advised. Major credit cards accepted. On King's Square (phone: 297-1522 or 293-9704).

Wharf Tavern A breezy *Somers Wharf* pub offering sandwiches, burgers, pizza, soup, and chowder at lunch, more substantial fare at dinner. The chefs' grill specializes in New England–style seafood dishes, and daily fish platters. Service can be slow. Open daily. Reservations unnecesary. MasterCard and Visa accepted. On *Somers Wharf* (phone: 297-1515).

INEXPENSIVE

Reid's A few steps from of the center of town, this is a casual place known for its mussel pie and fish cakes. Open for lunch and early dinner only; closed Sundays. No reservations. No credit cards accepted. Mullet Bay Rd. (phone: 297-1039).

White Horse Tavern Guests enjoy the atmosphere more than the food or service in St. George's oldest tavern. However, the spicy fish chowder is well worth sampling, and the conch chowder and burgers are good, too. Closed *Christmas, Boxing Day* (December 26), and *New Year's Day*. No reservations. Major credit cards accepted. On the harbor in King's Square (phone: 297-1838).

HAMILTON PARISH

EXPENSIVE

Plantation A congenial countryside setting for sampling Bermudian specialties, especially rich fish chowder and lobster in season. Plantation salad, homemade profiteroles (cream puffs filled with ice cream and topped with hot chocolate sauce), and Irish coffee are tasty, too. Closed Sunday lunch. Reservations necessary. Major credit cards accepted. Next to *Leamington Caves* in Bailey's Bay (phone: 293-1188).

Tom Moore's Tavern Here are several elegant dining rooms, with stone walls, wood beams, and fireplaces, in a historic 17th-century house. Impeccable service complements a surprisingly full continental menu—duck is a specialty, as is Bermuda lobster in season, and boneless quail in puff pastry stuffed with foie gras and served in cassis sauce. There's also an upstairs bar. Closed from mid-January through February. Reservations necessary. Major credit cards accepted. Adjacent to Walsingham Bay (phone: 293-8020).

Bailey's Ice Cream Parlour The place for all-natural treats, including ice cream, fruit sorbets (in summer), sandwiches, and other light fare. Open daily. No reservations. Major credit cards accepted. The original is across from the *Swizzle Inn* at Blue Hole Hill (phone: 293-9333). There is also a branch on Front St. in Hamilton City (phone: 292-3703).

CITY OF HAMILTON

EXPENSIVE

Bombay Bicycle Club Elegant, authentic Indian food (the tandoori and curry dishes are excellent) served in an elegant, yet relaxed atmosphere. The reasonably priced buffet lunches are first-rate. Closed Saturday lunch and Sundays. Reservations advised. Major credit cards accepted. Upstairs at 75 Reid St. (phone: 292-0048).

Little Venice Veal is the specialty, featured in such traditional ways as Sorrento, Milanese, and *limone* (with lemons). Popular with Bermudian business folks for lunch. Open for dinner only on weekends. Reservations necessary. Major credit cards accepted. On Bermudiana Rd. (phone: 295-3503).

Monte Carlo Specializing in Mediterranean cooking, this European-style bistro boasts an intimate atmosphere and first-rate crêpes; pasta and pizza are also recommended. Closed Sundays. Reservations unnecessary. Major credit cards accepted. Victoria St. (phone: 295-5453).

Once Upon a Table This old Bermudian home, all prettied up with lace curtains, is one of the best places to dine in town. The menu tries for (and succeeds at) deliciously different touches without getting too tricky. Recommended: poached Bermuda fish in creamy champagne sauce, wahoo marinated in lemon and lime juice, rack of lamb, and pumpkin or raspberry soufflé. Closed *Christmas* and the Thursday before the first Monday in August, for the annual *Cup Match*. Reservations necessary. Major credit cards accepted. Serpentine Rd. (phone: 295-8585).

Port O' Call This elegant establishment—looking much like the dining salon of a luxury cruise liner—is a favorite among businesspeople. Owned by Fritz Reiter, the proprietor of the well-known *Lobster Pot* (see below), its specialties include escargots prepared according to Fritz's secret recipe, lobster and crabmeat ravioli, stuffed and baked hogfish, roast veal shank, venison (in winter), and nightly specials. The service is excellent. Closed Saturday lunch. Reservations advised. Major credit cards accepted. Front St. (phone: 295-5373).

Red Carpet Another favorite haunt of Bermudian business folks and politicians, it specializes in homemade pasta, seafood ravioli in champagne sauce, and veal scaloppine. Closed Sundays. Reservations necessary. Major credit cards accepted. Reid St. (phone: 292-6195).

Romanoff This dining spot is notable for its Russo-European elegance. Menu highlights include borscht, chicken Kiev, and a formidable tournedos flambé Alexandra. Closed Sundays. Reservations necessary. Major credit cards accepted. In the Imperial Building on Church St. (phone: 295-0333).

Chancery Wine Bar Southern French fare, featuring daily and seasonal specials (game in fall, shellfish in summer), is the draw here. Recommended are the baked camembert *dijonnaise* and the house p[aca]té; there's a large selection of wine and beer. Enjoy the trellised courtyard and dining room with its low vaulted ceilings and cellar atmosphere. Closed Sundays. Reservations necessary. Major credit cards accepted. Chancery La. off Front St. (phone: 295-5058).

Hog Penny Inside the paneled rooms of this cozy local tavern, draft beer and ale and informal lunches and dinners are served. Try bangers and mash (sausage and potatoes), other English specialties, or curry. Closed *Christmas*. Reservations advised. Major credit cards accepted. Burnaby St., half a block from Front St. (phone: 292-2534).

Lobster Pot Bermudians choose it for spicy conch chowder, mussels, lobster (native September until April, from Maine other times); the ubiquitous Bermuda fish does very nicely indeed. The atmosphere's informal, the value excellent. Best for lunch during a Hamilton shopping excursion. Closed Sundays; shorter hours during winter months. Reservations necessary. Major credit cards accepted. On Bermudiana Rd. (phone: 292-6898).

Ristorante Primavera Elegant ambience and first-rate Italian fare make for a pleasurable dining experience. Daily specials are offered, but be sure to sample the fresh pasta or veal dishes. Open daily; dinner only on weekends. Reservations advised. Major credit cards accepted. On Front St. West, across from *Waterloo House* (phone: 295-2167).

Rum Runners There's the pub with a balcony overlooking the harbor for lunch and the Lord Halifax Room for more substantial lunches and dinners. Both have Watney's on tap and loyal local followings. Also, live entertainment nightly and satellite TV. Open daily from 10 AM to 1 AM. Reservations advised. Major credit cards accepted. Across from ship terminal No. 6 on Front St. (phone: 292-4737).

Show Bizz If you lived in Bermuda, this casual spot, with its small dining nooks and ceiling fans, would be your local place. On the menu are chicken wings, nachos, fish chowder, burgers, and short ribs. English Sunday brunch also is served. Entertainment includes music videos of top performers, including Whitney Houston, Lionel Richie, and Anita Baker (not too loud, either); a guitarist takes requests and a jukebox plays music of the 1950s, 1960s, and 1970s. Closed Saturday lunch. Reservations advised. Major credit cards accepted. On King St. at Reid (phone: 292-0676).

INEXPENSIVE

Fourways Gourmet Store A member of the famous *Fourways* family, this is a nice place to stop for breakfast, a light lunch, or afternoon tea. Enjoy a fine selection of delicious baked goods, salad, pizza, and hot dishes in a comfortable café setting. Closed Sundays. No reservations. Major credit cards accepted. On the ground floor of *Windsor Place,* on Queen St. (phone: 295-4085).

Fourways Pastry Shop This popular coffee shop (owned by the seemingly ubiquitous *Fourways* folks) boasts freshly baked breads, pastries, and croissants that are delivered from the parent establishment (in Paget) each day. Large windows facing the busy street make people watching a favorite pastime for customers having breakfast, lunch, or an afternoon snack. Stop in for coffee, tea, and sandwiches or sweets. Closed Sundays. No reservations. Major credit cards accepted. Reid St. (phone: 295-3263).

Pasta Basta An informal Italian cafeteria-style eatery with excellent daily specials; takeout, too. It's popular with locals. Open daily; dinner only on weekends. No reservations. Major credit cards accepted. On Eliot St. (phone: 295-9785).

Portofino For a quick, informal lunch, this small Italian café has the island's best pizza and pasta. Open daily; dinner only on weekends. Reservations advised. No credit cards accepted. On Bermudiana Rd., just down the street from the fancier *Little Venice* (phone: 292-2375).

Rose's Cantina The island's only Tex-Mex eatery. Chefs from Texas and Kentucky create delectable *fajitas,* enchiladas, and burritos. Closed Sunday lunch. No reservations. Major credit cards accepted. Reid St. (phone: 295-1912).

La Trattoria Reasonably priced, this informal Italian eatery features homemade pasta; pizza is tops, too. There's good cappuccino to top off your meal. Closed Sundays. Reservations advised. Major credit cards accepted. On Washington La. (phone: 295-1877).

SMITH'S PARISH

MODERATE

Inlet At the *Palmetto* hotel, breakfast, lunch and dinner are served in the dining room or on the terrace overlooking Flatts Inlet. The Bermuda fish chowder has won culinary competitions, and the English shepherd's pie and batter-fried Bermuda fish and chips are very popular choices. Sunday brunch is also delicious. Open daily. Reservations advised. Major credit cards accepted. Flatts Village (phone: 293-2323).

Halfway House In picturesque Flatts Village, across the water from the aquarium, this informal eatery serves breakfast, lunch, and dinner. At breakfast, the pastries are fresh from the oven; a Bermuda codfish breakfast is served on Sundays. A Caesar salad or a *croque-monsieur* (Swiss cheese, ham, and tomato on whole wheat toast) for lunch are good choices, as are fish chowder, and pan-fried Bermuda fish. There are also daily specials. Open daily. No reservations. Major credit cards accepted. Flatts Village (phone: 295-5212).

PAGET PARISH

EXPENSIVE

Fourways One of Bermuda's best restaurants (with good, but sometimes slow, service), it's set in one of the island's oldest buildings, built in 1727. The predominantly French menu includes excellent seafood, lamb, and veal dishes. The fish chowder is superb. There's both indoor and outdoor dining, and a snug bar. The piano music alone is a reason to visit. Open daily for dinner; Sunday calypso brunch; lunch served other days. Reservations necessary 1 or 2 days in advance. Major credit cards accepted. Where Cobb's Hill Rd. crosses Middle Rd. (phone: 236-6517).

Horizons Dinner on the terrace or in the dining room at this Relais & Châteaux cottage colony is among the island's premier culinary experiences. The seafood is highly recommended, particularly scallops in vanilla sauce, fresh Bermuda tuna with tomato, onion and olive oil, and salmon—grilled or poached to perfection. Be sure to leave room for the apple tart. Open daily. Reservations necessary (far in advance). No credit cards accepted. Paget West (phone: 236-0048).

MODERATE

'Brellas Casual dining under umbrellas on a terrace overlooking Hamilton Harbour. Cold fruit soup, fish chowder, and spinach salad are wonderful hot-weather refreshers. Entrées include tasty fresh Bermuda fish, either poached or grilled, and accompanied by Chef Neasley's Bermuda cassava pie with fresh vegetables. There's evening entertainment. Open June through early October. Reservations advised. Major credit cards accepted. At the *Newstead Hotel,* on Harbour Rd. (phone: 236-6060).

INEXPENSIVE

Paraquet A home-style, family restaurant patronized by local residents, this is the place to experience a typical Bermudian breakfast of codfish, potatoes, and bananas (served on Sundays only), as well as other local specialties and traditional American favorites. Open daily 9:30 AM to 1:30 AM. No reservations. Major credit cards accepted. On South Rd., not far from the *Elbow Beach* hotel (phone: 238-9678).

WARWICK PARISH

INEXPENSIVE

Paw Paw's This European bistro with separate French and Bermudian menus and a terrace overlooking South Road serves lunch and dinner. Stop in for a bite on the way to or from the beach. Closed Tuesdays. No reservations. Major credit cards accepted. On South Rd. on the way to Long Bay Beach (phone: 236-7459).

SOUTHAMPTON PARISH

EXPENSIVE

Coconuts Dining is a pleasure under a thatch roof overlooking pink beaches and blue water. The menu features nightly specials, including delicious cold fruit soups. The grilled seafood, chicken, and steaks are expertly prepared, and beautifully presented. Closed Sundays and from November through early May. Reservations necessary between 7 and 9 PM. No credit cards accepted. At the *Reefs Hotel,* South Shore (phone: 238-0222).

Henry VIII Features English and Bermudian fare (mussel pie, steak and kidney pie, roast sirloin, Yorkshire pudding), but with the strictly à la carte menu, the dinner check can average more than $75 per person with cocktails and wine. (Most patrons agree that the oversize portion of prime ribs and Yorkshire pudding is not to be missed—at any price.) The bar is always busy and draws convivial crowds for after-dinner piano entertainment. Wear smart casual attire. Closed *Christmas.* Reservations necessary. Major credit cards accepted. On the South Rd. across from the *Sonesta Beach* hotel (phone: 238-0908 or 238-1977).

Waterlot In a restored inn on the water (run by the adjoining *Southampton Princess* hotel), this dining room has its own dock for lunchers arriving by boat or ferry from the *Hamilton Princess.* The food, the site, the candlelit atmosphere are all elegantly evocative. Order anything (we suggest Bermuda fish or beef tenderloin with fried shallots and Brouilly wine sauce) with wine to match. There's a generous brunch buffet on Sundays (including first class Dixieland jazz). Reserve brunch well ahead, and ask for the second seating (around 1 PM) so you can linger. Closed January through April; open daily the rest of the year. Reservations necessary. Major credit cards accepted. On Middle Rd. near Riddell's Bay (phone: 238-0510).

SANDYS PARISH

EXPENSIVE

Cambridge Beaches Chef Jean-Claude Garzia blends the influences of his native Nice with Bermuda's freshest ingredients, including homegrown vegetables and herbs. The menu (which changes seasonally) offers what may well be the best food on the island; try the grilled wahoo served with a grapefruit and wine sauce or the filet of sole stuffed with spinach. If the hotel is full, it may be difficult for non-guests to get in, but it's definitely worth a try. Open daily. Reservations necessary. Major credit cards accepted. On Cambridge Rd. in Somerset (phone: 234-0331).

Lantana Colony Club A fine dining room known for its service, style, and wine cellar, in a flowery solarium (part of the elegant cottage colony). Highlights include a well-executed continental menu, and a lovely tradition of serving after-dinner coffee in the stylish *Meridian Lounge* or on the terrace. Open daily. Reservations necessary. No credit cards accepted. Between Somerset Bridge and *Fort Scaur* (phone: 234-0141).

Il Palio A local favorite that occupies a 2-story building just across from the *Somerset Cricket Club.* Italian specialties, including delicious pizza and first-rate pasta, are featured. Closed Mondays. Reservations advised (ask for an upstairs table by a window). Major credit cards accepted. Main Rd. on the southern outskirts of Somerset (phone: 234-1049).

MODERATE

Frog and Onion Housed in the historic Cooperage at the *Dockyard,* this charming pub-style eatery serves first-rate fish 'n' chips, lamb chops, and desserts. For lunch, try the leek and onion quiche. Closed November through March; open daily from noon to midnight the rest of the year. Reservations advised. Major credit cards accepted. *Dockyard,* opposite the *Craft Market* (phone: 234-2900).

Loyalty Inn Located in one of Somerset's beautifully restored historic buildings, this place is a must stop for fish dishes, especially mussel pie, fresh Bermuda fish, and the popular Somerset Sensation—seafood in a lobster bisque sauce over rice. Spectacular views of Mangrove Bay add to the ambience. Open daily; brunch served on Sundays. Pub food is available throughout the day. Reservations advised for Sunday brunch and dinner. Major credit cards accepted. Mangrove Bay Rd., Somerset (phone: 234-0125).

Somerset Country Squire A cheerful pub-restaurant that's especially jolly for lunch or dinner on the waterside terrace. The draft beer is a treat. Open daily. Reservations necessary. Major credit cards accepted. In Somerset, on Mangrove Bay (phone: 234-0105).

INEXPENSIVE

La Brioche One of Bermuda's best spots to savor espresso or cappuccino with a fresh pastry. Serves breakfast, morning tea, lunch (try the mini-pizza or quiche), and traditional English afternoon tea. Delicious ice-cream sundaes are available all day. Open daily (though its operating schedule is erratic during winter; call ahead). No reservations. Major credit cards accepted. In the *Clock Tower* at the *Dockyard* (phone: 234-1505).

Freeport The equivalent of a Bermuda diner, it's a relaxed spot to enjoy Bermuda fare with Bermudians. Try the homemade soup—especially the fish chowder—and fish sandwiches. Open for lunch and dinner daily; breakfast on weekdays. No reservations. Major credit cards accepted. Just inside the gate at the *Dockyard* (phone: 234-1692).

Diversions

Exceptional Pleasures and Treasures

Quintessential Bermuda

The best thing about Bermuda is that it's dependable. No high-rises will ever exceed eight stories, no visitors will ever drive cars. You can't see pastel houses dotting rolling green hills too many times; you just never tire of sunning on Horseshoe Beach; you won't ever fail to stare in awe at the sight of a cruise ship "parking" at a streetside dock in Hamilton. But whether this is your first or hundredth visit to Bermuda, the following are things we think you should know, places you should visit—and revisit—and uniquely Bermudian experiences that you just shouldn't miss.

ST. PETER'S CHURCH, St. George's If we had to choose just one place to express the essence of old Bermuda, it would be *St. Peter's Church* in the town of St. George's. This austere, whitewashed building is on York Street, just north of King's Square. The original church, the oldest Anglican place of worship in the Western Hemisphere, was built in 1612 and has virtually disappeared. Most of the building visitable today dates from the 18th and 19th centuries. Worn brick steps lead to the varnished cedar doors that open onto the nave, which is supported with great beams of native cedar. The upper gallery was built for slaves, who were forced by law to attend Anglican services throughout much of the 17th and 18th centuries. The two brass chandeliers that hang above the central aisle were donated in 1815 by two bitter political rivals: the Mayor of St. George's and the Governor of Bermuda. The three-tiered pulpit is carved from native cedar; so is the altar, which was built under the supervision of Governor Richard Moore in 1612. The vestry holds many fine examples of English silver, including a Charles I chalice probably donated by the Bermuda Company in 1625. The tablets that line the walls offer a lesson in the island's history: Note the memorial to Governor William Campbell, who died of fever only a few days after he set foot on the island. Wander through the churchyard, which is shaded by the belfry tree, said to be Bermuda's oldest cedar. Many of the gravestones are more than 300 years old. Among them stands the tomb of Midshipman Richard Dale, an American naval officer mortally wounded during the War of 1812; his epitaph includes a message from his parents, who praised the residents of St. George's for nursing their son as best they could. To the west of the main churchyard are the graves of slaves, some marked by headstones bearing only first names.

SOMERSET BRIDGE, Sandys Said to be the world's smallest drawbridge, this picturesque span links Bermuda's main island to the island of Somerset. The bridge can be drawn open 18 inches—just wide enough to let the mast of a sailboat slip through. It's most photogenic in the summer, when the pink and yellow oleanders on the bank are in bloom; stand on the grassy verge east of the bridge for the best view. If you look west from the bridge you'll see Ely's Harbour, a sheltered spot that was once a refuge for smugglers. To the east are the calm blue waters of the Great Sound.

A BERMUDA BUGGY RIDE If you're unabashedly romantic and haven't been discouraged by the surly coachmen in New York's Central Park, hire a carriage to ride through the aristocratic neighborhoods of Hamilton. Until 1946, when automobiles first invaded Bermuda's quiet streets, nearly every well-to-do family owned a couple of Morgans or Arabians and a surrey, roundabout, or brougham. Even the mail was delivered in this decorous manner, in a carriage known to locals as an Irish Jaunting Car. If you have a spare hour or two, go to Front Street in Hamilton, where a row of surreys awaits under an awning between the poinciana and ficus trees. Take a ride through Point Shares or Fairylands, just outside Hamilton, on a calm midmorning or midafternoon or on a warm summer evening, when the scent of jasmine and frangipani fills the air.

THE LONG AND SHORTS OF IT First-time visitors to Bermuda are usually nonplussed at the sight of businessmen walking down Front Street, briefcases in hand, dressed in jackets and ties—and shorts. In fact, these practical trousers have been an essential part of every Bermudian man's wardrobe since the 1920s. Their origins can be traced back to the early 20th century, when officers of the army of King Edward VII modified their uniforms to adjust to the island's balmy climate. The shorts those men wore were hardly as gay as the ones displayed in the shops along Front Street today; they were drably colored and baggy, and belted tightly at the waist. Tailors in Hamilton soon improved upon the original design, and the shorts—worn with cotton knee socks, loafers, a shirt and tie, and a blazer—became the standard uniform of Bermudian businessmen. During the 1930s, a law was passed to ensure that the shorts didn't violate local standards of propriety; the proper length was fixed at 2 to 4 inches above the knee. Policemen armed with tape measures patrolled the streets, and men caught wearing pants that fell short of the acceptable length were issued a warning.

Today, shorts have become a local trademark. From May to November, the warmest months of the year, they are worn by policemen, postmen, and waiters—and you may even see them at formal dinners or in church. They're still barred in some settings, however. You'll never see a whitewigged barrister dressed in shorts, and members of the Bermuda House of Assembly are prohibited from wearing them when Parliament is in session.

BERMUDA BREAKFAST If you're fortunate enough to wangle an invitation to a native Bermudian's home on a Sunday morning, you may be served the traditional, hearty, Sabbath fare of boiled salt cod, new potatoes, and slices of avocado and banana, topped with a cream sauce enriched with eggs. Some homes may offer cod hash made with tomatoes. It really doesn't matter; either version is guaranteed to please. Though it is now considered a major ritual on any self-respecting Bermudian's social schedule, the salt cod breakfast tradition was established among pre-refrigeration-age settlers for whom the easily preserved fish was a dietary staple. Though it's not the same as sampling the real thing, a savory—and more accessible—rendition can be enjoyed at the *Paraquet* restaurant on South Road in Paget and *Halfway House* in Flatts Village (for details, see *Eating Out* in THE ISLAND).

A WHALE OF A TIME If you'd like to tool around Bermuda's uninhabited isles, secluded coves, and coral reefs, rent a Boston Whaler with an outboard engine. The powerful little boats—descendants of those used as whaling boats off the coast of New England—are ideal for a personalized tour of Bermuda's waterways. To explore the western reaches of the island, duck under Somerset Bridge into Ely's Harbour and visit Cathedral Rocks just to the north; then head north toward the sleepy village of Somerset, where you can get a closer look at the islands just off Mangrove Bay. Around St. George's, fish for snapper in the waters of Castle Harbour and explore the 17th- and 18th-century forts on Castle and Charles Islands. The swell there can be strong, so be sure to anchor on the west side of the islands, toward the harbor. Avoid Nonsuch Island just to the north, for it's part of a nature reserve for cahows, a rare variety of petrel. Boston Whalers can be rented at *Rance's Boatyard* (Crow La., Paget; phone: 809-292-1843); *Robinson's Charter Boat Marina* (Somerset Bridge, Sandys; phone: 809-234-0709 or 809-238-9408); *Mangrove Marina* (Cambridge Rd., Mangrove Bay, Somerset; phone: 809-234-0914 or 809-234-0331, ext. 295); and *South Side Scuba Water Sports* (at *Grotto Bay Beach* hotel, Hamilton Parish; phone: 809-293-2915).

MOONGATE MAGIC These graceful circular stone arches—their origins and legends are drawn from the Chinese—can be seen at the entrances to homes, in gardens, and on rural byways all around Bermuda. Stand under one and make a wish—it's an obligatory ritual for tourists, particularly honeymooners. The island's oldest moongate is at the western entrance to *Par-la-Ville Gardens* in the city of Hamilton. It was built around 1920 by the Duke of Westminster's gardener, who was hired to landscape the area around the former *Bermudiana* hotel by Furness Withy & Co. Ltd., an English shipping firm that invested heavily in the island's tourist industry. Though no one has proof of this, moongates supposedly bring good fortune, and judging by their numbers, it seems that most Bermudians aren't taking any chances.

WHAT'S HOT If you've had a tough day of cycling or snorkeling, revive yourself with a bowl of fish chowder spiced with hot red pepper sauce and black rum. You also can sample tangy conch (pronounced "conk") chowder subtly seasoned with curry. The *Lobster Pot,* on Bermudiana Road in the city of Hamilton, serves both; while you're there, chat with the head bartender, Edwin Robinson, an expert in local lore (also see *Eating Out* in THE ISLAND).

RIDING A MOPED Bermudians call them motor-assisted bikes, and you'll find them for rent all over the island. They'll haul you up Bermuda's many hills with a minimum of effort, but make sure to take a thorough lesson in how to ride them before setting off—rental outlets are required by law to give instruction—and be sure to practice making several turns from the left-hand side of the road. Despite the official 20 mph speed limit, all too many tourists have suffered accidents by driving mopeds too fast. Save yourself the humiliation of being branded with "road rash"—the local term for the abrasions and scrapes suffered in moped accidents. You don't need a driver's license to rent one, but you must be over 16, and you must wear a helmet while riding.

GOING TO BAT If you visit during the summer, be sure to catch a cricket match. Imported by British soldiers in the 1840s, the game has inflamed local passions ever since. Eleven-member teams dressed in white uniforms compete on a grassy field (the "pitch"); the batter must run between the wickets (the set of three "stumps") to score. If you don't understand the odd terminology–you're likely to hear the words "silly mid-on," "maiden over," and "gulley" bandied about—ask the spectator next to you, and you're sure to get a friendly explanation.

Try to make it to the *Cup Match Cricket Festival,* which has been held in late July or early August each year since 1902. There you can watch two teams—*St. George's* and *Somerset,* representing the eastern and western sections of the island—battle it out. The 2-day event is an official holiday; shops close and government workers take the day off. Well-dressed crowds converge on the grounds, steaming plates of curried mussels and fish cakes are consumed, and men try their luck at the card game known as "Crown and Anchor"—it's the only time of the year when gambling is formally sanctioned in Bermuda. The *Bermuda Department of Tourism* (see *Tourist Information* in THE ISLAND) can provide the schedules for this and other matches.

SHOPPING FOR SHETLANDS There's no need to cross the Atlantic to shop for Shetlands. You'll find dozens of varieties of the sweaters in the stores along Front Street in Hamilton—and though the quality may not be quite as high as in years gone by, we won't quibble. There are styles made from Shetland, merino, and lamb's wool, as well as mohair, cashmere, and angora. The selection is virtually overwhelming: one store, *Archie Brown & Son,* stocks

30,000 sweaters. There's also a good selection at the many branches of *Trimingham's, Smith's,* and the *English Sports Shop,* as well as at *Marks & Spencer* on Reid Street in Hamilton. If you prefer a small but discriminating selection, stop in at the *Scottish Wool Shop* on Queen Street, Hamilton, just up from Heyl's Corner. In St. George's, visit *Taylor's* on Water Street. If you're in Bermuda in early January, take advantage of the annual sales, when sweaters can be purchased at unbelievably low prices.

GOMBEY DANCERS If you're visiting Bermuda around *Christmas* or *Easter,* you may see a group of masked dancers in fringed and spangled costumes frantically beating drums and running through the usually quiet streets. Don't be alarmed. As any local can explain, it's only the Gombeys. Their name is derived from the Bantu word for rhythm, and the dance they perform—usually on holidays or for special private celebrations—was invented in the 17th century by Bermudian slaves. The dance is part West African, part Caribbean, and part American Indian, for the Pequot Indians brought from New England to Bermuda as captured slaves or indentured servants in the mid-17th century left their mark on it, too. A mask painted with eyes, nose, and mouth conceals each dancer's identity; this may have been deliberate, for during the early colonial era the dances may have parodied the relationship between master and slave. Over the years, the dance lost its original meaning and new influences have crept in: notice the curious–perhaps entirely coincidental—resemblance to break dancing, and the Nikes and Adidas worn by some of the dancers.

BERMUDA BEAT For a taste of Bermuda's martial past, be sure to watch a Beat Retreat. This colorful ceremony takes place three times a month from April to October in several locations: on Front Street in Hamilton, in King's Square in St. George's, and at the *Royal Naval Dockyard.* (During the winter months, which locals call Rendezvous Time, watch the special "skirling ceremony" on Wednesdays at *Fort Hamilton*.)

The ceremony has its roots in a 17th-century ritual observed by British soldiers stationed on the island. At nightfall, troops were called back to their garrisons by a roll of drums—which became known as the beat retreat. Over the years, the ceremony grew increasingly elaborate, rather like the Changing of the Guard at *Buckingham Palace.* The band of the *Bermuda Regiment,* accompanied by the *Bermuda Islands Pipe Band* and the *Bermuda Police Pipe Band,* dressed in red, white, and blue tunics and white pith helmets, play martial music, and women dressed in kilts perform what looks like an English contredanse to the skirl of Scottish bagpipes.

GO FLY A KITE If you happen to be in Bermuda on *Good Friday,* you have a treat in store. After a breakfast of hot cross buns—an English tradition—head for Horseshoe Bay Beach in Southampton Parish. As you round the hill just north of the beach, you'll see hundreds of kites of brightly colored tissue paper flying in the breeze. This is the *Kite Festival,* which has been held every year since 1971. According to custom, the wooden frames of the kites are made in the shape of a cross; the kites are said to symbolize Christ's ascent to heaven. Prizes are awarded for the largest and smallest kites, which must be hexagonal shaped and made of wood and tissue paper. The largest among them span 12 feet and take 6 men to fly; the smallest may be only a half-inch across. If you're going to be in Bermuda at this time, it might be a good idea to plan ahead; visitors are welcome to compete. And while you're there, you can join a tug-of-war match or watch a group of Gombey dancers perform on the beach.

ALL THAT JAZZ If you want to see where Bermudian society turns out on a Sunday morning, reserve a dockside table at the *Waterlot* in Southampton. For decades, this has been *the* spot where Bermudians go for Sunday brunch (when they're not at home nibbling on a salt cod breakfast, that is). The food at the lavish buffet is quite good, and you should wash it down with a rum swizzle or a "dark 'n' stormy," made of black rum and ginger beer. For dessert, choose from the many varieties of chocolate cake, assorted pastries, and the flambéed strawberries. While you dine in this particularly picturesque setting, the natives will be pulling up to the dock in their launches or on the ferry to listen to the Dixieland beat of the *Somers Isles Jazz Band.* There are two sittings, at 11:30 AM and 1 PM; the second is preferable because you can linger until the band stops playing (around 3 PM). Brunch is served from May through December (for additional details, see *Eating Out* in THE ISLAND).

A Few of Our Favorite Things

Though Bermuda boasts plenty of fine hotels, spectacular beaches, and great golf courses, we've singled out a few select spots that are guaranteed to delight pursuers of a variety of pleasures. Follow our lead; we promise you won't be disappointed.

Each place listed below is described in greater detail in the island chapter.

SPECIAL HAVENS

The following are our special favorites for a stay in Bermuda. One is a larger, self-contained resort, others are small and intimate, but each in its own way offers the highest caliber of service, food, and island ambience. Complete information about our choices can be found on pages 52 to 55 of THE ISLAND chapter.

Cambridge Beaches, Somerset
Horizons, Paget
Lantana Colony Club, Somerset
Newstead, Paget
Reefs, Southampton
Southampton Princess, Southampton

BEST IN BOATS

With its perfect climate and crystal-clear waters, Bermuda is an ideal spot for boating. The following is a list of the best charter companies on the island. Complete information about our choices can be found on page 43 of THE ISLAND chapter.

Bermuda Caribbean Yacht Charter
Longtail Cruises
Mangrove Bay Marina
Ocean Yacht Charters
Sail Bermuda
Salt Kettle Boat Rentals
Sand Dollar Cruises
Starlight Sailing Cruises

TOP TEE-OFF SPOTS

Teeing off in Bermuda combines the best of two worlds: gorgeous island scenery and Great Britain's long-standing tradition of golfing excellence. The courses listed below—our particular favorites—are among the best in the world; any one of them will satisfy even the most demanding player. Complete information about our choices can be found on pages 44 to 45 of THE ISLAND chapter.

Belmont, Warwick
Mid Ocean, St. George's
Port Royal, Southampton
Riddell's Bay, Southampton

DREAM BEACHES

Bermuda is one of the world's best sun and swim places—and we think these nine stretches of beach deliver the ultimate combination of pink sand and turquoise sea. And as most of these places haven't yet been discovered by the masses, you may even be able to enjoy the much sought-after but often elusive gift of solitude. Complete information about our choices can be found on pages 48 to 49 of THE ISLAND chapter.

Astwood Cove, Warwick
Church Bay, Southampton
Elbow Beach, Paget
Horseshoe Bay, Southampton
John Smith's Bay, Smith's
Natural Arches, St. George's
Somerset Long Bay, Sandys
Spanish Point Park, Pembroke
Warwick Long Bay, Warwick

CHOICE COURTS

There's something about Bermuda's gentle sea breezes and warm sunshine that offers a matchless setting for tennis buffs. The clubs below offer all that an ace (or an amateur) could hope for—fine facilities, scenic backdrops, and all the extras. Complete information about our choices can be found on pages 49 to 50 of THE ISLAND chapter.

Coral Beach, Paget
Elbow Beach, Paget
Government Tennis Stadium, Hamilton
Grotto Bay Beach, Hamilton
Marriot's Castle Harbour, St. George's
Southampton Princess, Southampton

Historic Homes and Gardens

Bermuda's calm gentility is reflected in its historic homes and gardens. Many are preserved by the *Bermuda National Trust;* others are tucked away in obscure places and must be sought out. Some of the loveliest gardens on the island are private; to catch a good glimpse of them, it's best to climb on a bus and sit on the left-hand side.

The homes owned by the trust (phone: 809-236-6483) are open to the public daily year-round (unless otherwise indicated, there's an admission charge except for children under 12). The trust also arranges occasional tours of private houses and gardens. Silver-service coffees and teas and champagne receptions are offered at several homes, including *Verdmont* and *Tucker House,* now a museum. These receptions are only available to groups, however, and cost as much as $400 per group. If you wish to visit more than one *Bermuda National Trust* museum, ask for the special discount available to *Tucker House, Verdmont,* and the *Confederate Museum.* Also, since winter hours are often shorter, be sure to check times with the trust.

If you come to Bermuda during the spring, you may be able to see some of the island's finest homes and gardens on tours run by the *Garden Club of Bermuda.* Every Wednesday during April and May, the club offers tours of two or three houses. (For information, contact the *Garden Club of Bermuda,* PO Box HM 1141, Hamilton HMEX, Bermuda; phone: 809-295-1301.) The following are Bermuda's most lovely historic homes and gardens, listed alphabetically.

BARR'S BAY PARK, City of Hamilton This placid park, located a quarter of a mile west from the city's main shopping area, has a grand view of the waterfront. The docks of the *Royal Bermuda Yacht Club* are just to the left, and you can watch ferries, cruise ships, and sailboats slip in and out of the harbor. At night, you can relax here and watch the moon rise.

CAMDEN, Paget The official residence of the Premier of Bermuda, this stately white house stands amid carefully tended gardens off South and Berry Hill Roads. It was built in the early 18th century as a private home, and many prominent Bermudian families—the Joneses, Durhams, and Tuckers, among others—have lived in it. The Tuckers sold it to the Bermuda government, and in 1966 the property was annexed to the *Botanical Gardens of Bermuda,* creating a 36-acre park.

The house, whose two-tiered verandahs afford fine ocean views, has been renovated and rebuilt several times. It became the premier's official residence in 1979, but is used only for formal entertaining. Panels of native cedar carved in the mid-19th century line the entrance hall and dining room. The Victorian dining-room furniture is also made of local cedar, which has become increasingly rare. A 17th-century William and Mary mirror hangs above the dining-room fireplace, and a Hepplewhite desk and an 18th-century Sheraton console table stand in the drawing room. The walls are adorned with porcelain plates hand-painted with native flowers and 19th-century watercolors depicting Bermudian scenes.

Near the house stands a factory where arrowroot was processed; starch from the plant was exported during the 18th and 19th centuries to Europe and North America, where it was sought after as a thickener. You also can see carefully tended beds of ferns, roses, oleanders, and succulents. To reach the *Botanical Gardens,* walk westward across the parking lot (for information on the gardens, see *Natural Wonderlands* in this section). Maps of the property can be obtained from the *Department of Agriculture* office near the entrance to Point Finger Road.

The house is open to the public (unless an official function is being held) on Tuesday and Friday afternoons. No admission charge (phone: 809-236-5732).

CARTER HOUSE, St. David's Island Built between 1640 and 1650, this is Bermuda's oldest surviving stone dwelling. It was home for many years to descendants of Christopher Carter, one of the island's earliest settlers. Today, it is located on the grounds of the US Naval Air Station. A short flight of limestone steps leads to the varnished cedar door. The sagging gabled roof is original. Guides will point out the massive cedar beams and the kitchen fireplace where wild hogs once were hung to smoke. The house is furnished with prize pieces of 17th-century Bermuda cedar, and the library houses a collection of books about local history. A crafts fair is held here every September or October in conjunction with the base's air show. Visitors entering the base must show picture identification, and moped riders must wear a protective helmet and goggles while on the grounds. A *McDonald's* on the base serves the only "Big Macs" in Bermuda. The house is open Wednesdays. No admission charge, but donations are accepted. For information, call the curator, Mrs. Lyndell O'Dea (phone: 809-297-1150), or, on Wednesdays only, the guides at the house (phone: 809-293-5303).

OLD RECTORY, St. George's Located a stone's throw from the north entrance to *St. Peter's Church* on Broad Alley, this delightful Bermuda cottage, built in 1705, was home to the rector for only a few years. Its neat front garden faces a narrow macadam street. Thatch probably covered the original roof, which is now paved with slate. Remnants of the original half-timbered walls can still be seen. The cottage is furnished with many fine pieces of Bermuda cedar, including a four-poster bed. The property of the *Bermuda National Trust,* it is open to the public Wednesday afternoons. No admission charge, but donations are accepted. For further information, call the trust (see above).

PALM GROVE, Devonshire This 18-acre park, which extends from Middle Road to the island's southern coast, was developed by Bermudian entrepreneur Edmund Graham Gibbons, who purchased the property in the early 1950s. Once a working farm, it has been transformed into one of Bermuda's most spectacular gardens.

Magnificent stands of native trees—cedars, boxwoods, and fiddlewoods—shade the immaculate grounds. Rare palms shelter the old English statuary not far from the stone moongate, where lovers can make a wish for happiness. You can see more than a dozen varieties of palm trees, including princess, palmetto, bamboo, coconut, bottle, spindle, sago, and three kinds of date palms. More than 40 kinds of hibiscus bloom nearby. In a lily pond on the southern edge of the gardens is an 80-foot map of Bermuda designed by Gibbons and executed in concrete and clipped grass.

Tropical birds roost in the trees and call from large wire cages. You can see Brazilian macaws, South American toucans, Senegalese parrots, Australian rose-breasted cockatoos, Mexican aracari, and gray parrots from the Congo. Special nesting spots have been built for rare eastern bluebirds, which are enjoying a comeback, thanks to the efforts of the *Bermuda Audubon Society* and the *Bermuda National Trust.*

Visitors are encouraged to wander through the gardens, but are cautioned not to touch the plants. The property along the shore is closed to the public. The gardens are closed Fridays through Sundays. No admission charge (phone: 809-236-8144).

PALMETTO HOUSE, Devonshire This 18th-century limestone house is owned by the *Bermuda National Trust.* Its cruciform plan, which may have been designed to ward off evil spirits, is typical of many Bermudian homes of this era. Mullion windows look out on the North Shore. Fine specimens of cedar furniture can be seen in the three rooms open to the public. During the 19th century the house was used by members of the golf course run by the British garrison at Prospect Camp. It is open to the public on Thursdays. No admission charge (phone: 809-295-9941).

PAR-LA-VILLE GARDENS, BERMUDA LIBRARY, BERMUDA HISTORICAL SOCIETY, City of Hamilton If you need a shopping break, head for this gracious old mansion surrounded by a 2½-acre park. The property once belonged to William

Perot, the island's first postmaster. An enormous rubber tree dominates the garden's Queen Street entrance; Perot, who collected exotic plants from all over the world, planted it in 1847. Mark Twain, a frequent visitor to the island, was said to have been disappointed that the tree didn't "bear a crop of hot water bottles and rubber overshoes." If you walk out to the Bermudiana Road entrance of the park, you'll see the oldest moongate on the island (see *Quintessential Bermuda* in this section).

On a warm day, you can relax and read on the upstairs verandah of the house or inspect the collection of the *Bermuda Historical Society Museum,* which includes 17th- and 18th-century Bermuda silver, 18th-century china, antique cedar furniture, "hog money" (Bermudian coins engraved with pictures of wild hogs, which used to roam the island in the early days), and a copy of the letter from George Washington in 1775 requesting that Bermuda ship gunpowder to his troops. A sea chest belonging to Admiral Sir George Somers stands in the entrance hall, and a 17th-century portrait of him and Lady Winifred, his wife, hangs on the wall. There are also models of early settlers' ships and a handsome display of 19th-century watercolors.

The park is open daily; the library and museum are closed Sundays. No admission charge (phone: 809-295-2905, library; 809-295-2487, museum).

POINT PLEASANT PARK, City of Hamilton Located just behind the Bank of Bermuda near the ferry terminal, this pocket-size park, better known as *Albouy's Point,* provides an excellent view of the tugboats that guide the great cruise ships to their moorings. Ships dock here Mondays, Tuesdays, and Wednesdays from May through October. Liners usually dock between 8:30 and 10 AM. Freighters and container ships unload their cargo from here, too. Bring a picnic brunch and spend a pleasant hour or two.

SOMERS GARDENS, St. George's This park is the site of the tomb where the heart of Admiral Sir George Somers was buried in 1610 (his body lies in Lyme Regis, England); the vault is recessed into the wall to the left of the entrance. Carefully tended flowers bloom beneath tall royal palms, and there are plenty of benches on which strollers can drowse on a sultry afternoon.

STATE HOUSE, St. George's Completed in 1620, this is the island's oldest stone building. Bermudian magistrates and assemblymen convened here for 200 years until the capital was moved to Hamilton. Its massive limestone blocks are cemented together with mortar made from turtle oil and lime. Since 1815, it has been let to the island's Freemasons, who pay a modest rent: one peppercorn a year. The fee is handed over to the Governor of Bermuda with great ceremony every April. Located on Princess Street, the *State House* is generally open Wednesdays, but it's best to check the schedule with the visitors' service bureau in St. George's (phone: 809-297-1642).

TUCKER HOUSE, St. George's This simple whitewashed structure, built in 1711, is linked to many historical events. Henry Tucker, President of the Governor's Council, lived here from 1770 to 1808. He had occupied the house for only a few years when a family quarrel broke out. In 1775, his father, Colonel Henry Tucker, defied British orders by smuggling gunpowder to the American colonies. This didn't sit well with the younger Henry's father-in-law, Governor James Bruere, a staunch Loyalist.

Portraits of Henry Tucker's family, painted by English artist Joseph Blackburn, hang on the walls of the house. There are also specimens of 18th-century Bermudian and English furniture, the Tucker family silver, and a handsome collection of antique needlework. Guides will explain that the kitchen once doubled as the barbershop of Joseph Hayne Rainey, a freed American slave who became the first black member of the US House of Representatives; Barber's Alley is named for him. While Rainey was trimming beards, his wife sewed dresses for many of St. George's wealthy matrons. The house is closed Sundays. Admission charge (phone: 809-297-0999).

VERDMONT, Smith's This is a must. Now owned by the *Bermuda National Trust,* this manor was built in 1710, probably by prominent shipowner John Dickinson. The house was never modernized; its most recent resident, Miss Lillian Joell (who lived here until 1951), dipped water from the cistern outside, lit oil lamps at night, and cooked on a kerosene stove. If you walk through the rose gardens on the south side of the house, you'll be rewarded by the fine vistas of the coast. The first entrance to the house was on this side; if you look up, you'll see that the original mullion windows are still intact. On the west side of the house is a garden planted with herbs and flowers that might have been cultivated here in the 18th century.

The clean scent of cedar fills the house; the staircase, with its graceful balustrade and elaborately carved newels, is made of the wood. Brick fireplaces adorn all eight rooms; the upstairs floors are finished with broad cedar planking and pitch pine from the Carolinas. The 18th-century cedar furniture–including a drawing room desk, a William and Mary tallboy, several chests, and a tea table in the library—are in beautiful condition. The English cabinets filled with rare Chinese porcelain are made of mahogany; so are the two 19th-century pianos. Children will enjoy the antique toys in the nursery, including an odd 19th-century tricycle designed to be pedaled with the hands. The museum is closed Sundays (phone: 809-236-7369).

VICTORIA PARK, City of Hamilton This jewel of a park is three blocks north of Front Street, directly behind *City Hall.* Sunken gardens planted with oleanders and flowers surround a graceful silver-painted bandstand, erected in the 1880s to celebrate the *Golden Jubilee* of Queen Victoria's reign. In the days when British soldiers billeted on the island, the park rang with martial music. Today it's peaceful and silent, unless you're lucky enough to hear an impromptu concert.

Touring Bermuda's Forts

Virtually every strategic point along Bermuda's coastline is guarded by a fort, and many of them are worth a visit, both for their impressive views and for the tangible sense they give of the island's history. Only a few served any real strategic purpose; British fears of American bellicosity proved largely unfounded, and the massive cannons and 12-inch guns on the island have long been silent.

English settlers on St. George's Island were the first to fortify the colony; their crude wooden stockades, built around 1612, successfully repelled foreign interlopers, particularly the Spanish. As time passed, garrisons sprang up in western Bermuda as well, and the early wooden structures were replaced by sturdy bastions built of native limestone. With the outbreak of the American Revolutionary War, the Royal Navy strengthened its presence on and around the colony. Old forts were refurbished and new ones built. Construction continued during the 19th century, when the Royal Navy made Bermuda its western North Atlantic headquarters, earning the colony the name "Gibraltar of the West." The following is a survey of Bermuda's most notable bastions. Unless otherwise indicated, all are open daily and don't charge admission.

ALEXANDRA BATTERY, St. George's Located just off Barry Road, this fortress was built in the mid-1860s to protect a vital shipping channel into St. George's Harbour. It was named for Princess Alexandra of Denmark, who married the Prince of Wales in 1863. The battery overlooks Buildings Bay, where the survivors of the wreck of the *Sea Venture* made one of the ships in which they continued their voyage to Virginia in 1610 (no phone).

DEVONSHIRE BAY BATTERY, Devonshire The ruins of this battery, built in 1616 to defend the south shore, stand not far from Spanish Rock. The site is easily accessible from South Road and affords impressive views of the Atlantic. During World War I, a group of German soldiers from the merchant raider *Krönprinzessin Victoria Louise* came ashore here—the only time in the history of Bermuda when an enemy landed on the island (no phone).

FORT HAMILTON, Pembroke Towering over Hamilton Harbour and the surrounding parishes of Paget, Devonshire, and Pembroke, this fort was built between 1866 and 1889. Its inception dates from more than 10 years earlier, as part of the Duke of Wellington's grand design for the fortification of Bermuda. The need for a stronger defense became increasingly clear following the American Civil War, as Bermudians realized how vulnerable they would be should another large-scale conflict occur. From its garrisons, British soldiers kept close watch over the roads leading to the capital and to Spanish Point, where the admiral lived. There are 18-ton guns and a drawbridge that spans its 50-foot moat. Visitors can wander the length of the moat now; it's planted with allspice trees, five varieties of palms, and orchids (no phone).

FORT ST. CATHERINE, St. George's Located northwest of *Alexandra Battery,* this fort is one of the island's earliest strongholds. Built in the 17th century under the supervision of Richard Moore, Bermuda's first governor, it was enlarged 200 years later, largely with convict labor. It sits on a point overlooking a strategic channel near the beach where survivors of the wreck of the *Sea Venture* stumbled ashore in 1609. A drawbridge spans a grassy moat, and the hillside is riddled with tunnels and secret chambers. The museum within houses dioramas depicting the island's history, plus replicas of the Crown Jewels of England and an impressive cache of ammunition (phone: 809-297-1920).

FORT SCAUR, Sandys The British Navy built several fortresses to secure vulnerable routes to the *Royal Naval Dockyard.* This fort, near Somerset Bridge in Sandys Parish, was built in 1865 to protect the dockyard from a southern assault. It overlooks the Great Sound to the south of the dockyard, and commands a fine view of Somerset Island. Its soldiers never saw battle, however, and it gradually fell into disrepair; much of its artillery has been dismantled by the British. US Marines billeted nearby during World War II. From the ramparts you can look across the Great Sound to Spanish Point, where the Admiral of the *Dockyard* fleet once lived; if you look through the telescope on a fair day you can see *St. David's Lighthouse* on the northeastern tip of Bermuda, 14 miles away. Guides will explain the complex workings of the disappearing carriage on which the fort's cannon sat (phone: 809-234-0908).

FORT WILLIAM, St. George's Just over the crest of Government Hill Road north of St. George's stands this 19th-century redoubt, built on the ruins of *Warwick Castle.* Visitors can wander through the passageways that lead to the old magazines and storerooms (no phone).

GATES FORT, St. George's A small 17th-century stronghold, it stands a quarter of a mile south of the *Alexandra Battery.* Visitors can explore the ruins of its three-gun battery and magazine (phone: 809-297-1920).

MARTELLO TOWER, St. George's This garrison was designed to bar enemy ships sailing into Ferry Reach and St. George's Harbour. Located on the western tip of St. George's Island, it was built in 1823 from native limestone. The 18-pound gun atop the tower rotated 360 degrees. A military graveyard and the remnants of a railway run by the John Jacob Astor family can be seen nearby (no phone).

ROYAL NAVAL DOCKYARD, Sandys Located at the northern tip of Ireland Island, this bastion was the boldest British venture on Bermuda. Once the largest naval base in the western Atlantic, it is still the colony's most impressive fortification. Royal engineers drew up plans for its massive breakwaters, wharves, boat slips, barracks, and keep during the tense years preceding the War of 1812. Ground was broken on the site in 1809, and over the next two decades thousands of slaves and British convicts labored here under appalling conditions; many died of yellow fever.

After hostilities broke out in 1812, a British fleet set off from the dockyard to launch a successful attack on Washington, DC; the seige resulted in the burning and sacking of President James Madison's White House. Not surprisingly, much of the loot from this escapade ended up in Bermuda. Over the next 150 years, the dockyard bustled with activity; during the late 19th century, it employed several thousand men. As time passed, square-rigged frigates and fast corvettes were replaced by ironclads and steam-driven dreadnoughts; cannons were left to rust, replaced by torpedoes and shells. During World War I, five Royal Navy armored cruisers were stationed here to protect British ships from German vessels, and during World War II Allied submarines and destroyers stopped at the dockyard for servicing and repairs.

The most impressive structure here is the old keep, next to the *Bermuda Maritime Museum.* Visitors cross the moat over a concrete drawbridge and enter through an archway in the casemate walls, which are 20 feet thick in some sections. Thirty-foot ramparts surround the keep, and a visitor can see its labyrinthine storage chambers, water gate, and inner lagoon, where sailors loaded munitions into dinghies to take to ships waiting offshore. The adjacent ordnance buildings are admirably constructed; notice their vaulted brick ceilings, whitewashed limestone walls, and floors coated with spark-resistant bitumen. The oldest ordnance building has been converted into an exhibition hall; you can see models of old pilot boats and cruise liners, as well as treasures dredged from the *San Antonio* and the *San Pedro,* Spanish galleons wrecked off the reefs west of Bermuda in the late 16th and early 17th centuries.

Near the keep stands the *Boatloft.* Built in 1853, it now houses a collection of ships made on the island, including a fully rigged 19th-century dinghy, the *Victory,* and a 42-foot pilot gig. Craft such as these sailed far out to sea to guide incoming vessels past Bermuda's treacherous reefs. Here you also can see the dockyard's turret clock, made in 1856; its 9-foot pendulum marks perfect time, and three bronze bells ring out the hours. Also nearby is the *Commissioner's House,* which was completed in 1830. Its occupants lived well, judging from its furnishings: Mahogany paneling lined the rooms, which were fitted with marble fireplaces and baths; the stable housed 11 horses, and there was room for several carriages. The office of commissioner was abolished only 10 years later—in an effort, most likely, to eliminate graft—and the mansion was converted into a warehouse. It is now being restored to house museum exhibits.

The great floating dock that accommodated the Royal Navy's ships has now disappeared. The original dock, made of massive iron plates, was towed from England to Bermuda in 1868; at the time, it was the largest in the world. The dock was replaced and enlarged twice. During World War II, more than 500 Allied ships docked here for repairs. The dock was dismantled in 1972 (phone: 809-234-1418 for general information).

ST. DAVID'S BATTERY, St. George's In the northeastern part of St. David's Island is a pair of 9.2-inch guns that once propelled shells 20 miles out to sea—quite a technological feat for the time. One of the most modern fortifications on the island, *St. David's* was completed in 1910 and was manned by American forces during World War II (no phone).

WHALE BAY BATTERY, Southampton This fortification, which stands near the western edge of Southampton Parish, was built to stave off ships bound toward Hog Fish Cut, a channel to the south of the *Royal Naval Dockyard*. Visitors can explore its ruined ammunition magazine and barracks or scramble down the cliffside paths to the beach (no phone).

Natural Wonderlands

To most urban dwellers, the island world is one vast natural wonder—a serendipitous embrace of land, sea, and sun that is wide enough to include anyone who ventures into the area. And they aren't all that wrong. But even in paradise there are superlatives, and the spots below give a special sense of Bermuda's special splendor.

BOTANICAL GARDENS OF BERMUDA, Paget The thousands of trees, shrubs, vegetables, and flowers that bloom here year-round have been a source of education and enchantment for Bermudians and visitors since 1898. Every shape, color, and scent under the sun thrives in these 36 beautifully tended acres; in the *Garden of the Blind,* you can close your eyes and have your remaining senses feast on myriad aromatic spices and herbs. While wandering through the hibiscus patch you will come across most of the 150 varieties of hibiscus that thrive on the island. The formal gardens may make you feel as though you've strolled into an Impressionist painting. By the time you've reached the cactus collection and the vegetable plot, your head will be buzzing with botanical questions, while your psyche enjoys a satisfying sense of contentment. In good weather, volunteers conduct highly informative, free guided tours from 10:30 AM to noon on Tuesdays, Wednesdays and Fridays from April through October; Tuesdays and Fridays from November through March. Tours leave from the gardens' *Visitors' Service Centre,* near the Berry Hill Road entrance. The center also has a gift shop and a café. The *Botanical Gardens* are at *Camden,* between Berry Hill and South Roads in Paget Parish (see also *Historic Homes and Gardens* in this section). The gardens are open daily from sunrise to sunset. No admission charge. For more information, contact the *Department of Agriculture* (phone: 809-236-4201).

CAVES, Hamilton Bermuda's natural caves are spectacular wonders, too. Guided tours, although commercially oriented, are given in *Crystal Caves* (phone: 809-293-0640), off Wilkinson Avenue in Hamilton Parish, and in nearby

Leamington Caves (no phone), on Harrington Sound Road. In both cave complexes, there are spectacular stalagmites and stalactites—the fairyland-like formations created by the buildup over millions of years of calcite and calcium crystals. *Crystal Caves* are closed in December and January; open daily the rest of the year. *Leamington Caves* are open daily year-round. Admission charge for both.

IDWAL HUGHES NATURE RESERVE, Hamilton The *Bermuda National Trust* is attempting to restore the native forest and exotic plant life in the 22-acre *Walsingham Trust. The Idwal Hughes Nature Reserve,* part of the *Walsingham Trust* property, off Harrington Sound Road, can be entered by driving down the road to *Tom Moore's Tavern.* The trail starts to the left of the restaurant, and runs about three-quarters of a mile. There's a three-acre lake fringed with mangroves—and some natural caves. About a quarter of a mile farther is the "blue pool"—a refreshing place to take a swim. At *Walsingham Glade* is the stump of a calabash tree where Irish poet Tom Moore is said to have composed many of his verses. The *National Trust* has planted another tree on the same site. Open daily. No admission charge. For more information about these sites, contact the *Bermuda National Trust* (see above).

NATURE'S SCULPTURES Dramatic cliffs and craggy formations of coral and limestone can be seen along most of the island's southern coastal beaches. Among the most spectacular are the Natural Archs, the 35-foot-high limestone formations at Mid Ocean Beach in Tucker's Town. At Stonehole Bay (between Jobson's Cove and Chaplin Bay in Warwick), there is a naturally eroded hole in a rock that towers over the picturesque bay. If you're out in a boat, go to Ely's Harbour to see Cathedral Rocks across from Cathedral Island, near Somerset Bridge.

SPITTAL POND, Smith's Another of Bermuda's natural wonders, this is a seaside nature reserve where as many as 500 varieties of birds spend the winter and where dozens of species of North American waterfowl sojourn during migration. Although the pond is fenced off, the undeveloped and enormously varied acreage surrounding it is open to the public. To preserve this special piece of wild, unmanicured Bermuda, do as the sign instructs and stick to the nature trails and footpaths. Cross sections of the cliffs—nesting places for native Bermuda sea birds—provide a living history of the ocean's ebb and flow for over 200,000 years. The *Department of Agriculture* (see above) offers guided tours of the refuge. Open daily. No admission charge. South Shore, Smith's Parish.

UNDERWATER WONDERS The coral reefs and dramatic coastline afford visitors an entirely different view of Bermuda. Corals, shells, and the seemingly endless varieties of colorful fish that fill Bermuda's waters make each dive memorable. (For information on Bermuda's best underwater spots, see *Snorkeling and Scuba* in THE ISLAND.)

Taking to the Water

GLASS-BOTTOM BOATS

Some of the finest views of Bermuda's marine life can be seen from a glass-bottom boat. The best excursions visit shipwrecks several miles offshore. Generally, the farther you go from shore, the better the visibility; if you're lucky, you can see down 150 feet. There are even four-hour cruises that include an hour or two of snorkeling. Crews provide life vests for non-swimmers and will cheerfully instruct novice snorkelers; equipment is included. Joffre Pitman, owner of *Pitman's Snorkeling* (at Somerset Bridge; phone: 809-234-0700), has learned a good deal about marine ecology during his 30 years at sea. His 44-foot *Fathom* has an ample 19-by-4-foot viewing glass. Snorkelers can also make the trip in the 54-foot launch operated by *Hayward's Snorkeling & Glass Bottom Boat Cruises* (phone: 809-292-8652, day; 809-236-9894, night); underwater cameras can be rented on board. *Reef Roamers* (phone: 809-292-8652) also offers a two-hour cruise.

FERRIES

Taking a ferry isn't just an inexpensive and practical way to see the island. It's a great way to get a taste of how the locals live. Ever since the island's only passenger railway closed down in 1948, Bermudians have relied on ferries and buses to get around. Hop on a ferry from Hamilton around 5:30 in the evening, and you're likely to see groups of businessmen dressed in Bermuda shorts, ties, and blazers discussing the day's commerce. Many of them are accompanied by bicycles so they can pedal home from their ferry stop. If you're riding a ferry around 3:30 on a weekday afternoon, you'll be joined by crowds of uniformed schoolchildren. Ferries are great social levelers; you'll see maids in starched white uniforms elbow to elbow with tennis pros and restaurateurs.

From the ferry you'll also have a backyard view of some of the finest homes on the island, many of which are barely visible from the street. It's also the perfect place from which to catch a glimpse of the launches and sailboats tied up along private docks and see gardeners trimming hibiscus hedges and poinciana.

The ferries run daily from Hamilton to Warwick, Paget, and Somerset. The Hamilton ferries leave from the terminal next to the visitors' service bureau on Front Street. If you like, combine a walking tour with a trip by ferry or bus. For instance, take the ferry to Cavello Bay in Somerset, walk three-quarters of a mile along East Shore Road to Somerset Village, then take the bus back to Hamilton. You'll need exact change for the bus; fares vary depending on exactly where you're going. You can pick up a copy of bus and ferry schedules in Hamilton at the *Ferry Terminal* on Front Street or the bus depot on Washington Street next to the *City Hall*. The visitors' service bureaus in Hamilton, St. George's, and the *Royal Naval Dockyard* also have schedules. Here's what to look for along selected ferry routes:

HAMILTON TO PAGET On this ride to Paget, you can look across Harbour Road at *Bentley,* a chestnut-colored mansion built in 1630, and *Casa Rosa,* the 18th-century house next door. Just before the ferry reaches Hodson's Landing, you'll see *Girvan,* a pink two-story house built in the 1920s upon cliffs that drop 30 feet into the harbor. Next to it is *Overlook,* a brown-and-white home built around the turn of the century; note the eyebrow moldings over the windows. On the far side of Hodson's Landing is *The Moorings,* which was built as a sea captain's warehouse in the 18th century. Just beyond it lie the green cottages and grand manor house of *Newstead,* one of Bermuda's best small hotels. Farther down is *Paget Hall,* a pale blue mansion built around the turn of the century; it's the largest home along this stretch of shoreline. The ferry stops at Salt Kettle, a secluded cove where traders once unloaded salt from the Turks Islands; looking down the bay you'll see *Stanwick,* a rust-colored cottage with green shutters and gabled slate roof.

WARWICK TO HAMILTON Along this route you'll see *Kempdon,* a yellow home surrounded by terraces landscaped with ferns and palmetto trees. To the east, across Salt Kettle Bay, stands *The Chimneys,* a rose-colored 17th-century home with six—count them—six chimneys. To the west is Hinson's Island, site of many luxurious homes; if you get off here, you can get a good look at the yachts and private launches in the little bay on the south side of the island. As you near Hamilton, the grand estates of *Point Shares* and *Fairylands* swing into view.

HAMILTON TO SOMERSET If you should take the ferry ride to Somerset, you'll pass the Somerset drawbridge (see *Quintessential Bermuda* in this section); just beyond it is the annex to the US Naval Air Station (the main air base is on St. David's). Past that, just before *Fort Scaur,* is *The Parapet,* a yellow mansion built by an American family earlier in this century. Cottages tumble down the hillside at the picturesque Cavello Bay ferry stop; the large white house at the end of the point looks like a typical 18th-century Bermudian farmhouse, though it was built within the last decade. As the ferry pulls in to the *Royal Naval Dockyard,* you'll see the 19th-century row houses that once belonged to officers of the Royal Navy.

Sunken and Buried Treasure

Bermuda's treacherous reefs have threatened the skill of knowledgeable navigators since the earliest explorers neared its shores, and more than 300 wrecks have been discovered around the archipelago. But many ships that met their fate off the island lie undiscovered and untouched. And visions of days gone by are easy to imagine, particularly when walking through the island's strategically situated fortresses that are sprinkled around the coasts, or when taking a close look at the relics from the wrecks that are displayed in the *Bermuda Maritime Museum*'s Treasure House (see *Museums* in THE ISLAND).

Dating back to the 16th century, Spanish and Portuguese ships—laden with gold and silver—thought Bermuda would make a safe harbor. Often grossly miscalculating their positions, they crashed on the then-uncharted coral reefs. The island's waters saw plenty of action during the 16th and 17th centuries, when Bermudian privateers were chased by envious pirates wanting to relieve them of their valuable cargoes. And Union ships boldly came to the island in an unsuccessful attempt to stop Bermudian blockade runners from successfully landing Confederate cotton and taking valuable English arms to the South. The Royal Navy was very strong in Bermuda, and beginning in 1792 the *Royal Naval Dockyard* at Bermuda's western end became a most important base, often referred to as the "Gibraltar of the West."

If you discover a wreck and want to protect your find, register with the Receiver of Wrecks in Hamilton. What follows are some of the protected open-dive sites that can be explored off Bermuda.

The *Constellation* area, as well as wrecks of the *Kate, Minnie Breslauer, Hermes, Rita Zoretta,* and *Pelinaion,* are sanctuaries protected under the 1990 Fisheries (Protected Areas) Order. It is an offense to damage or remove anything from them. A yellow buoy marks each site and should be used for mooring; if a boat is already tethered to it, set your anchor in the sand to avoid damaging the coral reefs.

An unusual configuration of two wrecks from different eras make the *Constellation* area, near Western Blue Cut (about 7 miles west of Somerset), a historically rich dive site. Here lies the *Montana,* an English paddle-wheel steamer, that had been heading for the Confederate states with precious English cargo during the height of the blockade-running in 1863. The *Constellation,* an American four-masted schooner under the command of Capt. Howard Neves, sank in 1943 while carrying cement and supplies to La Guaira, Venezuela. Huge sacks of cement are still strewn across the ocean floor.

In December of 1873, the *Kate* sank off the island's east end, near Mid Ocean Beach in Tucker's Town. Under the command of Capt. James Simpson, it was carrying a large cargo of cotton destined for Le Havre, France. It lies close to shore.

The wreckage of the *Minnie Breslauer,* which went down in 1873 on her maiden voyage, sits about a mile and a half off Long Bay, Warwick. A steamer cargo ship that had crossed the seas from Lisbon, Portugal, it was carrying dried fruit, cork, and lead that was to have been delivered to New York.

Joining the *Minnie Breslauer* in its watery grave in 1985 under very different circumstances is the *Hermes.* Abandoned by a bankrupt foreign company, it was intentionally sunk by the *Bermuda Divers Association* to create a fish reef and dive site. Today, many colorful fish now call the *Hermes* home.

Two popular open-dive sites off St. David's Island are the *Rita Zoretta,* an Italian cargo steamer that sank in 1924, and the *Pelinaion,* a Greek cargo steamer that went down 16 years later.

Another popular dive spot is around *L'Herminie,* a 60-cannon French warship that sank in 1838 several miles west of Somerset while going from Cuba to Brest, France. It's easily accessible, and lies in about 35 feet of water.

The *Eagle* is an ancient wreck lying at North East Breakers; it sank in 1658. To its east is the "bead wreck"—so called because the name of the vessel isn't known. Around it, thousands of glass Indian trading beads lie strewn across the ocean floor. To its west, about 10 miles northeast of Bermuda and a mile and a half east of North Rock, is the *Cristóbal Colón,* a Spanish ship that went down in 1935 at the height of the Spanish Civil War. Local divers say that mysterious circumstances surround the sinking of this 10,600-ton steamer.

A Shutterbug's Bermuda

Despite its small size, Bermuda offers a lifetime of photographic treasures. Be it the hustle and bustle of shoppers on Front Street when the cruise ships are in, the flamboyantly costumed Gombey dancers at *Christmastime,* the incredible pink sand beaches that dot the island, or the other—and equally splendid–views from on board the ferry, memories are here, just waiting to be captured on film. Even a beginner can achieve remarkable results with a surprisingly basic set of lenses and filters or a camcorder. Equipment is, in fact, only as valuable as the imagination that puts it into use.

LANDSCAPES AND SEASCAPES The Bermuda landscape is of such quiet, yet compelling beauty that it is often the photographer's primary focus. Each of Bermuda's nine parishes has a personality all its own; and the sea views—either from on board a sailboat or a ferry—encompass a world of pastel houses, moongates, and turquoise blue waters.

Lighting is a vital component in landscapes and seascapes. Take advantage of the richer colors of early morning and late afternoon whenever possible. The overhead light of midday is often harsh and without the shadowing that can add to the drama of a scene. This is when a polarizer is used to best effect. Most polarizers come with a mark on the rotating ring. If you can aim at your subject and point that marker at the sun, the sun's rays are likely to be right for the polarizer to be effective. If not, stick to your skylight filter, underexposing slightly if the scene is particularly bright. Most light meters respond to an overall light balance, with the result that bright areas may appear burned out.

Although a standard 50mm to 55mm lens may work well in some landscape situations, most photographers will benefit from a 20mm to 28mm wide-angle lens. Hamilton Harbour, the *Royal Naval Dockyard,* and the *Botanical Gardens* are just some of the panoramas that fit beautifully into a wide-angle format, allowing not only the overview, but the opportunity to include people or other points of interest in the foreground. A flower, for instance, may be used to set off a view of *Par-la-Ville Gardens;* people can provide a sense of perspective in a shot of the *Clock Tower.*

To isolate specific elements of any scene, use your telephoto lens. Perhaps there's a particular carving on a doorway of historic *Camden* that would make a lovely shot, or it might be the interplay of light and shadow on the coral reefs at Horseshoe Bay. The successful use of a telephoto lens means developing your eye for detail.

PEOPLE As with taking pictures of people anywhere, there are going to be times in Bermuda when a camera is an intrusion. Consider your own reaction under similar circumstances, and you have an idea as to what would make others comfortable enough to be willing subjects. People are often sensitive to having a camera suddenly pointed at them, and a polite request, while getting you a share of refusals, will also provide a chance to shoot some wonderful portraits that capture the spirit of the island as surely as the scenery does. For candids, an excellent lens is a zoom telephoto in the 70mm to 210mm range; it allows you to remain unobtrusive while the telephoto lens draws the subject closer. For portraits, a telephoto can be used effectively as close as 5 to 7 feet.

For authenticity and variety, select a place likely to produce interesting subjects. Front Street is an obvious place for visitors, but if it's local color you're after, visit Paget, home to many of the island's local artists (there are some galleries here, too); wander along the railway trail; or go to one of the rocky North Shore beaches that are popular with locals. Aim for shots that tell what's different about Bermuda. In portraiture, there are several factors to keep in mind. Morning or afternoon light will add richness to skin tones. To avoid harsh facial shadows cast by direct sunlight, shoot where the light is diffused.

SUNSETS When shooting sunsets, keep in mind that brightness will distort meter readings. When composing a shot directly into the sun, frame the picture in the viewfinder so that only half of the sun is included. Read the meter, set, and shoot. Whenever there is this kind of unusual lighting, shoot a few frames in half-step increments, both over and under the meter reading. Bracketing, as this is called, can provide a range of images, the best of which may well be other than the one shot at the meter's recommended setting.

Use any lens for sunsets. A wide-angle is good when the sky is filled with color-streaked clouds, when the sun is partially hidden, or when you're close to an object that silhouettes dramatically against the sky.

Telephotos also produce wonderful silhouettes, either with the sun as a backdrop or against the palette of a brilliant sunset sky. Bracket again here. For the best silhouettes, wait 10 to 15 minutes after sunset. Unless using a very fast film, a tripod is recommended.

Orange, magenta, and split-filters are often used to accentuate a sunset's picture potential. Orange will help turn even a gray sky into something approaching a photogenic finale to the day, and can provide particularly beautiful shots linking the sky with the sun reflected on the ocean. If the sunset is already bold in hue, an orange filter will overwhelm the natural colors, as will a red filter—which can nonetheless produce dramatic, highly unrealistic results.

NIGHT If you think that picture possibilities end at sunset, you're presuming that night photography is the exclusive domain of the professional. If you've got a tripod, all you'll need is a cable release to attach to your camera to assure a steady exposure (which is often timed in minutes rather than fractions of a second).

For situations such as revues and other nighttime entertainments, a strobe does the trick, but beware: Flash units often are used improperly. You can't take a view of the Bermuda skyline with a flash. It may reach out as far as 30 feet, but that's it. On the other hand, a flash used too close to a subject may result in overexposure, resulting in a "blown out" effect. With most cameras, strobes will work with a maximum shutter speed of 1/125 or 1/250 of a second. If you set the exposure properly and shoot within range, you should come up with pretty sharp results.

CLOSE-UPS Whether of people or of such objects as flower blossoms, close-ups can add another dimension to your photography. There are a number of shooting options, one of which is to use a 70mm or a 210mm lens at its closest focusable distance. Unless you're working in bright sunlight, a tripod will be worthwhile. If you are very near your subject and there is a good deal of reflective light, it may pay to underexpose a bit in relation to the meter reading.

If you do not have a telephoto lens, you can still shoot close-ups using a set of magnification filters. Filter packs of one-, two-, and three-time magnification are available, converting your lens into a close-up lens. Even better is a special macro lens designed for close-up photography.

A SHORT PHOTOGRAPHIC TOUR

Here are some of Bermuda's most photogenic places.

FRONT STREET, Hamilton The best view of the capital city's pastel-colored skyline with its dramatic Gothic-style Anglican cathedral can be captured with a telephoto lens from the Paget public ferry dock at Lower Ferry or with a standard lens on any ferry en route to Hamilton. Another perspective of Hamilton is from the harbor side of Front Street, looking east from the "birdcage" at Heyl's Corner (at the *Irish Linen Shop*) at the rows of brightly colored striped awnings of the shops flapping gaily in the breeze; occasionally, there'll be a pith-helmeted policeman in Bermuda shorts directing traffic.

BOTANICAL GARDENS AND CAMDEN The 36 acres of meticulously manicured gardens include colorful displays of artistically arranged flower beds; though they change throughout the year, they are at their best in the spring. Also spectacular is the variety of colors in the formal rose gardens next to *Camden,* the official residence of the Premier of Bermuda. The best view of *Camden,* a stately, 18th-century house with sweeping lawns and towering trees, is from near the South Road entrance. The lighting is best in the early morning hours.

ST. PETER'S CHURCH, St. George's Nestled above a wide flight of brick steps on York Street, the oldest Anglican place of worship in the Western Hemisphere is a shutterbug special. The most dramatic shots can be taken with a wide-angle lens looking upward from the base of the steps. Also worthy of recording on film are the gravestones in the cemetery to the rear of the church. Their centuries-old, though fairly readable, inscriptions give silent testimony to the arduous lives of Bermuda's early settlers.

ST. GEORGE'S BACK STREETS Much of the history and charm of this early-17th-century town is best expressed in its back streets and alleyways. Here, along narrow cobblestone lanes such as Shinbone Alley, along the eastern side of Somers Gardens and Silk Alley, at the bottom of York Street, you will discover homes and storefronts still intact after hundreds of years. Try to frame your shots from the top—or bottom—of the alleyways for a total view, or, using a telephoto lens, focus on a specific building or shop. And though some might think it's a cliché by now, be sure to have your picture taken while you're "pilloried" in the 17th-century stocks on Kings Square in St. George's.

WARWICK LONG BAY Though it's difficult to single out any one best beach in Bermuda, for the camera buff, this strand has the most varied landscape. When seen from the South Road, the magnificent rock formations just off-shore, the dramatic hillside covered with Spanish bayonet and oleander, and the pristine pink sand are the stuff of which photographic dreams are made.

MOONGATE MAGIC Borrowed from the Chinese, but now a very Bermudian tradition, moongates—symbols of good luck and eternal love—can be seen at the entrances to homes and public lands throughout the island. The oldest, and most often photographed, is at the western end of *Par-la-Ville Gardens* in Hamilton. Honeymooners should get someone to take their picture while standing beneath a moongate. Just make a wish, smile, and let the moongate work its magic.

Directions

Introduction

It's probably just as well that visitors are not allowed to drive cars in Bermuda, for it's a place best explored at the slowest possible speed. A study in pastels, where houses have names like *Sunnylands* and *Verdmont* instead of 23 East Eighth Street, where perfectly manicured hedgerows are interrupted only by surprise bursts of fuchsia, the island is worthy of a long, leisurely stroll—or pedal. Here, it seems, there is time for everything: for lunching alfresco on a canopied terrace dining room, relaxing on a roadside bench, or swimming in a bright turquoise sea off one of the island's famous pink beaches. Every bend in a Bermuda road opens onto a new vista, and every detour brings a new discovery.

Each of the parishes—there are nine in all—has its own personality. History-rich St. George's is the site of the oldest Anglican church in the Western Hemisphere; Pembroke prides itself on its especially pastoral settings; Sandys (commonly called Somerset) has one of the island's most impressive forts. You can walk the same roads in Smith's where smugglers ran, watch golfers tee off in Southampton at one of the world's top courses, or duck into *Trimingham's* in Paget for a surprisingly inexpensive Shetland sweater. Take your time, and take the advice of locals, who say, "Just follow your nose."

No matter how you choose to explore the island, most of Bermuda's 21 square miles of rolling landscape is accessible to visitors. You can walk, bike, ride a moped or a bus, hire a driver, or hop on a ferry. Just remember, the rules of the road are different here: People walk and drive on the left, and the official speed limit is 20 mph (though it's often exceeded). If you walk on the main roads, be careful—few have sidewalks or shoulders.

For a thorough investigation of the island, there's no better way to get around than on two feet. Some of the best walking routes follow the old railway bed, which traverses the length of the island from Somerset to St. George's, excluding a 3-mile section around Hamilton that was converted into a highway years ago. Diesel-powered trains, operated by the *Bermuda Railway Company,* rattled along on this track from 1931 to 1948. The railroad, which took 25 years to build, cost more than £1 million—mile for mile, one of the most expensive in the world. But trains traveled the track for a mere 17 years. The railroad's 33 bridges, many of them built by Canadian Indians, corroded badly in the salt air and required constant repair. That, and the introduction of the automobile to the island (in 1946), led to the demise of the "Old Rattle and Shake." The track was torn up, and in 1984 the government opened the old railway route to pedestrians, horseback riders, and bicyclists. (Bermuda's old railroad cars are now chugging along tracks in Guyana—the former British Guiana.)

Hikers also can explore the network of tribe roads that link Bermuda's north and south shores. Many of these steep, narrow roads were built during the early 17th century, soon after Richard Norwood of the Bermuda Company surveyed the island. They were probably used to transport freight between cargo ships and the interior of the island. Cyclists also can travel along the generally steep tribe roads and the railway trail, but they must stop from time to time to lift their bikes over small metal barriers.

For a glimpse of the way Bermudians live, hop on a bus or ferry. You can eavesdrop on a group of schoolchildren talking about their next cricket match or listen to businessmen discussing the new fishing regulations. It's a great way to pick up the nuances of the local idiom. The pink public buses are inexpensive—it costs $3 (exact change required) to ride the longest route. Buses run frequently; wait for them by the pink and blue poles or weathered stone shelters along the roadsides. The seats are perched high off the ground, so you can peer over the hedgerows and get a good look through the signature moongates at some of the island's lovely private gardens. From this vantage point, you also can read the hand-painted signs announcing each house's name; Bermudians have observed this charming custom since the mid-17th century.

Ferries are the least expensive—and perhaps most enjoyable—form of local transportation. There's no better way to see the harbor or to catch a glimpse of native life (see *Taking to the Water* in DIVERSIONS). Bikes are allowed free on the ferry; there is an extra charge for mopeds.

If you're coordinated and agile, you may want to rent a moped (see *Moped Rental* in THE ISLAND). Be sure to wear comfortable clothes and rubber-soled shoes. Long pants and long sleeves are also advised (to guard against sunburned knees and arms), and a helmet is required by law. Leave your long scarves at home; you don't want anything to catch in the wheels.

And if you prefer to let someone else do the driving, there are several excellent drivers and guides for hire. They can take you to many out-of-the-way places, and they'll tailor the tour to your interests. Our favorite drivers are listed under *Taxi Touring* in THE ISLAND; if they're not available, you can hail any one of the taxis flying a blue flag from its hood (or bonnet, as the Bermudians say). The drivers of these vehicles have passed a government exam and are licensed to serve as tour guides.

On the following pages you will find tours through each of Bermuda's nine parishes; you'll see its forts, its waterways, and its historic homes and gardens. (All phone numbers listed in this section are in the 809 area code unless otherwise stated.) These outings, which can be enjoyed by hikers and/or cyclists, are presented in geographical order, from east to west. Enjoy—and remember, walk *and ride* on the left.

Strolling St. George's

Standing in the center of King's Square in St. George's—Bermuda's first capital and most history-rich parish—you have a sense of spanning several centuries at the same time. At the pier, a modern, 12-story cruise liner dwarfs the full-scale wooden replica of Sir George Somers's 17th-century ship the *Deliverance*. Shops selling T-shirts and other souvenirs stand near the cedar stocks and pillory once used to punish colonists for everything from missing church on Sunday to stealing a pig. Standing at the head of the square is the 17th-century *Town Hall,* where St. George's mayor and aldermen go about the business of government. Just to its right stands a modern, computerized tourism office.

As you follow the routes outlined below, you'll find that history and commercialism coexist well here. But to really capture the mood of St. George's, get here early. Before the shops open, the pace in the parish hearkens back to another time. You almost expect to find some sinner locked up in the stocks on the square, or see a horse-and-buggy "school bus" carrying children to class. Remember, you'll have plenty of time to shop later.

Our first route leads through the town, past some of the parish's historic forts. It's best to follow this trail on foot, for 400 years of history are compressed into St. George's narrow, winding streets, and you have to walk slowly and look carefully to take in all of it. Our second route leads to St. David's, a secluded island southeast of St. George's, and can be followed on foot or two wheels (except for the walking trail through *Great Head Park* and the path leading to the lighthouse). The last two routes—best covered on moped or bicycle—pass some lovely coves and historic forts.

ST. GEORGE'S OLDE TOWNE AND FORTS

The first tour starts right in the town, which was founded in 1612, soon after the first settlers arrived. Bermuda's courts and General Assembly met here until 1815, when the capital was transplanted to Hamilton. Square-rigged trading ships docked here in the 17th century, and during the American Civil War, sail-assisted steamships smuggled supplies to the Confederacy from a base in the *Globe* hotel on York Street.

Start from King's Square in the heart of the old city. Walk south across the square, past St. George's oldest pub, the *White Horse Tavern* (see *Eating Out* in THE ISLAND). On your return, sample their spicy fish chowder—with lots of dark rum and sherry peppers. Remember, when the cruise ships are in, shops and restaurants are crowded, and there is often a long wait for a table—especially one on the terrace. The chowder, however, is well worth the wait.

Cross the bridge to Ordnance Island, where there's an unobstructed

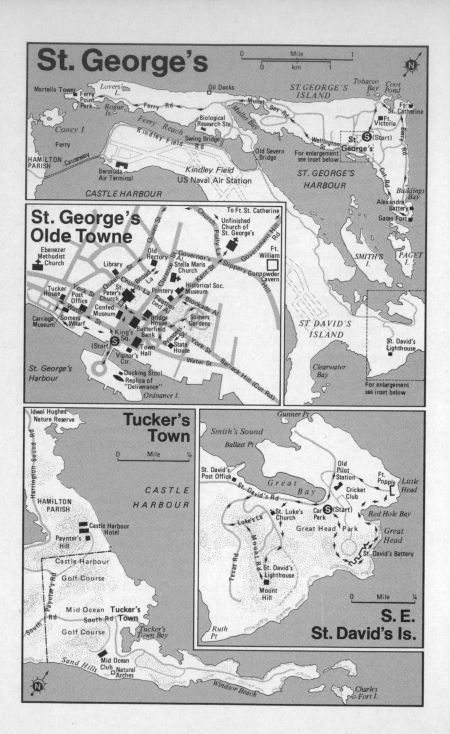

St. George's

Mile
km

Martello Tower
Lovers' L.
Ferry Point Park
Rogue Is.
Oil Docks
ST. GEORGE'S ISLAND
Tobacco Bay
Coot Pond
Ferry Rd
Muller Bay Rd
Muller Bay
Ft. Catherine
Ft. Victoria
Coney I.
Ferry Reach
Kindley Field
Swing Bridge Rd
Biological Research Sta.
Wellington St
St. George's (Start)
Berry Rd
HAMILTON PARISH
Causeway
Bermuda Air Terminal
Old Severn Bridge
For enlargement see inset below
Cut Rd
Kindley Field
US Naval Air Station
ST. GEORGE'S HARBOUR
Buildings Bay
Alexandra Battery
CASTLE HARBOUR
Gates Fort
SMITH'S I.
PAGET I.

St. George's Olde Towne

To Ft. St. Catherine
Unfinished Church of St. George's
Ebenezer Methodist Church
Church Folly
Government Hill Rd
Ft. William
Library
Old Rectory
Governor's Al
Stella Maris Church
Slippery Hill
Gunpowder Cavern
Queen St
Tucker House
York St
Queen St
St. Peter's Church
Broad La
Clarence St
Kent St
Printery
Historical Soc. Museum
Post Office
Ward St
Confed. Museum
Feather bed Al
Blockade Al
Somers Gardens
Carriage Museum
Somers Wharf
Bridge House
Butterfield Bank
Princess St
York St
Water St
Barrack Hill (Cut Rd)
St. George's Harbour
King's Sq.
(Start)
Town Hall
State House
Visitor's Ctr.
Ducking Stool
Replica of "Deliverance"
Ordnance I.

ST. DAVID'S ISLAND
For enlargement see inset below
St. David's Lighthouse
Clearwater Bay

Tucker's Town

Mile ½

Idwal Hughes Nature Reserve
Harrington Sound Rd
Smith's Sound
Ballast Pt
Gunner Pt
CASTLE HARBOUR
St. David's Post Office
St. David's Rd
Great Bay
Old Pilot Station
Cricket Club
Ft. Popple
Little Head
HAMILTON PARISH
St. David's Rd
St. Luke's Church
Car Park (Start)
Red Hole Bay
Castle Harbour Hotel
Paynter's Hill
Luke's La
Great Head Park
Great Head
Castle Harbour Golf Course
Paynter's Rd
Texas Rd
Mount Rd
St. David's Battery
Mid Ocean South Rd
Tucker's Town
St. David's Lighthouse
Mount Hill
South Rd
Tucker's Town Bay
Golf Course
Ruth Pt
Mile ¼
Sand Hills
Mid Ocean Club
Natural Arches
Windsor Beach
Charles Fort I.

S.E. St. David's Is.

view of the harbor—unless there's a cruise ship in port. During the 17th century, murderers were brought here to be hanged from the gibbet. There's also a ducking stool, used to punish lesser offenders. In the 18th century, the British Army stored munitions on the island. On your left is a replica of the *Deliverance,* one of two ships that carried survivors of the wreck of the *Sea Venture* to Jamestown, Virginia, in 1610. You can climb aboard the vessel (called *Deliverance II* by the locals) to appreciate just how cramped its passengers were. The ship is open daily; admission charge (phone: 297-1459). Just to the west stands a life-size bronze statue of Admiral Sir George Somers, the *Sea Venture*'s captain.

Cross the bridge back to the square; a few yards down on the right, past the 19th-century cannon, is the visitors' service bureau; staff members are available to answer questions Mondays through Saturdays (phone: 297-1642). To the east stands the reconstructed *Town Hall,* where St. George's mayor, aldermen, and councillors still preside; even the cedar woodwork is a faithful replica of the original. The meeting rooms are lined with portraits of all but two of St. George's mayors dating back to 1787 (the other two must have been camera—or palette—shy). A slide show about the island's history is shown upstairs Mondays through Saturdays; admission charge (phone: 297-0526).

On the north side of the square is *O'Malley's Pub on the Square,* which serves splendid grilled fish on the second-story verandah overlooking the square (see *Eating Out* in THE ISLAND). A few yards away are stocks and a pillory, where punishment was meted out to wayward citizens. Nearby is *Peniston-Brown* (phone: 297-1525), which sells French scents at duty-free prices, and branch offices of the Bank of Butterfield and the Bank of Bermuda.

Down Water Street to the west of the square is the post office; across the street is *Frangipani* (phone: 297-1357), a boutique that sells women's clothing from Greece and Guatemala. *Taylor's* (phone: 297-1626), a bit farther down on the left, carries a wide selection of British woolens, including kilts.

A few paces down is the *Carriage Museum,* with its handsome collection of 18th- and 19th-century carriages. Bermuda resisted entry into the Automobile Age until 1946, when a law was passed permitting cars on the island. Bermudians soon abandoned their surreys and barouches for luxurious Sunbeam Talbots, Morrises, and Austins. Fortunately, some of the finest early carriages were salvaged and are now on display in this pleasant setting. You can see mail "trucks," elegant black-fringed hearses, wagons for children, and a velvet-lined coach that makes you wish that automobiles still weren't permitted here. The museum is open weekdays; no admission charge (phone: 297-1367). The *Carriage House,* just one door down, specializes in pan-fried Bermuda fish topped with roasted almonds and bananas (see *Eating Out* in THE ISLAND).

Diagonally across the street to the right is the *Tucker House.* The former home of Henry Tucker, Bermuda's colonial secretary during the American Revolution, this small 18th-century cottage has a fine collection of furniture, silver, and Mrs. Tucker's jewelry. It is closed Sundays; admission charge (phone: 297-0999; also see *Historic Homes and Gardens* in DIVERSIONS). In the lower level of *Tucker House* is the *Book Cellar* (phone: 297-0448), where you can pick up a good novel or a book about Bermuda history.

There's a decent Italian restaurant, *San Giorgio* (phone: 297-1307), down on the right; try the veal scaloppine. The *Wharf Tavern,* on the left just at the end of the street, has good pub food—sandwiches, burgers, and fish and chips (see *Eating Out* in THE ISLAND). From there take a left and walk about 50 feet toward Hunter's Wharf. *Portcullis,* which sells family crests and pewter and stone chess sets, is hidden in the pink building on the right (you can reach the proprietor at his home; phone: 297-0952).

Backtrack toward King's Square along Somers Wharf. Once a warehouse district, this area has been refurbished, and several shops, including *Trimingham's* (phone: 297-1726) and *A. S. Cooper & Sons* (phone: 297-0925), have opened up here. You'll also find *Cow Polly East* (phone: 297-1514), which sells an eclectic mix of international clothes and gifts. Throughout this maze of shops, you'll catch glimpses of the turquoise sea just a few yards away on the right. Stop a while–sit down on a bench with a cool drink, and enjoy the view.

On York Street, just north of Water Street, is *St. Peter's Church,* one of the town's finest historical monuments (see *Quintessential Bermuda* in DIVERSIONS). As you climb its worn brick steps, you can imagine men in top hats and ladies in bonnets coming to worship on a Sunday morning. The splendid interior is enough to inspire even the severest skeptic. Be sure to visit the lovely cemetery in the back. Though most of the inscriptions on the tombstones, worn by age and the elements, are unreadable, you can still make out a few. One—*Here lieth the Body of Mrs. Mary Bell, Wife of Dr. Richard Bell, Who departed this life the 13th of March, 1793. Aged 17 years*— indicates the brief life span of the early settlers. (Tombstones of Mrs. Bell's two children, ages 2 years and 3 weeks respectively, are nearby.) Behind *St. Peter's,* just across Church Lane down Broad Alley, is the old stone-and-timber rectory. Originally *St. Peter's* parsonage, it was built in 1705 by a repentant pirate. The rectory is open to the public on Wednesday afternoons. *Note:* You'll probably want to make a return visit to *St. Peter's.* It's worth several hours' attention all by itself.

Across from the main entrance to *St. Peter's,* on the corner of York Street and King's Square, is the *Confederate Museum,* which is operated by the *Bermuda National Trust.* Located in the old *Globe* hotel, from which Confederate agents sent orders to Bermudian blockade runners who supplied the South during the Civil War, it contains a small collection of maps and other Civil War memorabilia. The museum is closed Sundays; admission charge (phone: 297-1423). If you stroll farther east down York Street and cross Kent Street, you'll see *Somers Gardens* on the left. A living tribute to Sir George Somers, the man who settled these islands in 1609, the gardens contain an array of exotic flowers and palm and other varieties of trees; it is also the place where Sir George's heart is buried (also see *Historic Homes and Gardens* in DIVERSIONS). The gardens are open daily; no admission charge for children under 12 (no phone).

If you walk from the gardens onto Blockade Alley and up Kent Street, you'll be rewarded with a splendid view of the town (some of the island's most beautiful flowers grow here). Less than 100 yards south on Princess Street, at the top of the hill, stands the white limestone *State House.* Dating from the 17th century and still in use today (it became a Masonic lodge in 1815, and its tenants–still Masons—pay the government a rental of one peppercorn a year, a payment tendered with great pomp and ceremony each April), it's the island's oldest stone building. It's usually open to the public on Wednesdays, but call before going over; no admission charge (phone: 297-1642). Nearby is a small walled garden containing a bust of Tom Moore, the Irish lawyer and poet who lived for a few years in Bermuda. *Bridge House,* a 17th-century colonial home owned by the *Bermuda National Trust,* is on the southwest corner of the park. Located here is the *Bridge House Art Gallery,* which exhibits a large collection of watercolors by local artists. It's open daily (phone: 297-8211).

Continue north on Kent Street and cross York to Featherbed Alley on the left. Go into the *Featherbed Alley Printery,* where there is a working 18th-century press and a replica of the one invented by Johannes Gutenberg in the 15th century. Be sure to look at the tiny kitchen in the rear. The printery is closed Sundays; no admission charge (phone: 297-0009). The same building is also home to the *St. George's Historical Society Museum,* which has a fine collection of Bermudian furniture, china, and silver (some of the latter is said to be the bounty of 17th-century sea captains' privateering raids). The museum is open weekdays; no admission charge for children under 6 (phone: 297-0423).

Continue up the steady incline of Kent Street until it joins Slippery Hill. Before you stands the ruin of *St. George's,* an Anglican church begun in the 19th century and later abandoned due to lack of funds and schisms among the congregation. It is known among locals as the "Unfinished Church." (Don't venture inside, as you might be hit by a piece of loose masonry!) There is a grand view of the old part of town from here, and you can see St. David's Island across the harbor.

From here you can walk left up Church Folly Lane for a quarter of a mile, turn left onto Queen Street, and walk down to York Street, where you can hail a bus or cab back to your hotel. If you'd like to continue on, you can pick up our St. David's Island route here (see below), or head out from the ruins of *St. George's* to *Fort St. Catherine* and *Gates Fort,* a walk of about 4 miles. It runs through level terrain, and it's well suited for bicycles and mopeds—if you don't mind a barking dog or two.

To take the fort route, turn left as you leave the church and walk up Government Hill Road, a continuation of Kent Street. After 300 yards or so, you'll pass *Fort William* on the right; inside the fort is *Gunpowder Cavern* (phone: 297-0904), a restaurant that stands atop some of the galleries where munitions once were stored. Walk along the 18-hole *St. George's Golf Club* (phone: 297-8067 or 297-8148), and you'll see a high-rise hotel (now unoccupied) on the right; bear left, and the road leads to the beaches at Tobacco Bay. Outcroppings of coral and limestone shelter the bay, and the water is shallow and calm—perfect for a midday swim. (There's a changing room and snack bar on the beach.)

From the bay, head northeast on Coot Pond Road to *Fort St. Catherine.* Be sure to allow enough time to stroll the ramparts and absorb the somber mood that permeates this stronghold (see *Touring Bermuda's Forts* in DIVERSIONS). Open daily; no admission charge. From there you can pick up Barry Road, which runs over barren and windswept hills past an 18th- and 19th-century military graveyard and some abandoned British naval garrisons to *Alexandra Battery.* The battery overlooks Buildings Bay, where Sir George Somers and his crew built the *Deliverance.* Pastel cottages line the remaining quarter mile to *Gates Fort* (phone: 297-1920). The fort, built circa 1615, is named after Sir Thomas Gates, who was shipwrecked along with Somers. From here you can look across the rocks to Horseshoe Island. Galleons sailed through this narrow channel during the 17th century, and the modern cruise ships that dock at St. George's pass this way, too.

Past *Gates Fort,* modern cottages line Cut Road to Barrack Hill (named for the presence until the 19th century of the British military; some 19th-century garrison buildings can be seen as you walk toward the Olde Towne). You'll pass the *St. George's Dinghy & Sports Club* about a quarter of a mile beyond the fort. Just down on the left is *The Palms,* a lemon-colored Victorian house with elaborate grillwork along the verandah, ornamental urns perched on the edge of the roof, and a widow's walk. On the last stretch of this tour, there's a fine view of the harbor and the old town. Bear left onto Water Street, which winds past several historic homes and leads back to King's Square. You can stop for that fish chowder now, do some shopping, and then catch the bus on York Street, across from the *Ebenezer Methodist Church,* or call a cab from King's Square (if you can't just flag one down).

ST. DAVID'S ISLAND

St. David's belongs to St. George's Parish, but its residents jokingly claim it's really the other way around, and that non-natives need a passport to land on the island. In fact, it was not until 1934 that St. David's Island was linked with the rest of Bermuda by the Severn Bridge. (That bridge, which connected the island to St. George's, is no longer standing; landfill, created during the construction of the nearby American military base in the 1940s, now connects the area to the mainland. The original bridge was named for a tunnel that connects St. David's county in Wales and St. George's county in Great Britain.)

Life in St. David's is quiet, and even the presence of the US Naval Air Station doesn't disturb things much, aside from the takeoffs. For the most part, life revolves around fishing and boat building, as it has for centuries. People of many races live side by side with a minimum of strife, as they do in other parts of Bermuda. Some of the island's families—including the Foxes, Pitchers, and Lambs—can trace their ancestry back to the Pequot Indians brought from New England by slave traders in the 17th century. You won't find any grand hotels or nightclubs on St. David's, but if you're looking for a down-home spot to savor a fine grilled rocktail or snapper, this is the place.

The following 4-mile walking tour begins at *Great Head Park* in the eastern corner of the island, just southeast of the cricket grounds. In the back of the parking lot is a series of stone steps leading into an area thickly wooded with cedars, palmettos, and cherry trees. Take this trail for about 200 yards and you'll reach a fork; bear right. Walk through the groves of fiddlewood and Australian pines, taking care not to stray from the path, for poison ivy flourishes here.

Soon you'll see the octagonal red-and-white tower of *St. David's Lighthouse,* in the distance to the southwest. The trail will fork again; bear left past a ruined garrison for a fine view of the Atlantic. Keep left as you make your way down the main trail, and in 100 yards or so there's a narrow path that plunges down to the edge of a cliff. If you're not afraid of heights, make your way down this trail to a point where you can see a large cave in the limestone cliffs across the cove. Then retrace your steps until you reach the main path, and continue on for another 100 yards or so until you meet a broad track. Take a right onto the track, which cuts through a dense thicket of fiddlewood and finally comes out in a high meadow overlooking Red Hole Bay.

As you cross the meadow you'll see the remnants of *St. David's Battery,* which was built in 1738. The rusting six- and nine-inch guns here were once among the finest in the British Empire. Walk to the chain-link fence at the eastern edge of the meadow; it's a sheer 150-foot drop from here to the ocean. (These are the highest cliffs in Bermuda.) You can pick up the trail near the gun farthest to your left as you face the ocean; follow it to the northern edge of the meadow. Don't wander from the path—there's plenty of poison ivy here, too. Midway down the hill is a tumbledown command post; at the bottom is a broad track that skirts the bay. Follow the track north past a cricket field and up a grassy ridge (several paths diverge here, so keep on the well-worn path in the middle).

On the other side of the ridge, near the shoreline, are the remains of a 19th-century fortification carved out of solid rock; notice the notches where cannon once protruded. Follow the track closest to the shore, past outcroppings of wind-stunted cedars. In a quarter of a mile or so, you'll come upon a group of mangroves sheltering a small cove; if you want to swim here, change clothes in the lavatories. Near the beach is *Dennis's Hideaway* (phone: 297-0044), a down-home seafood eatery run by Dennis Lamb. It's actually located in Lamb's home, and he prepares (and sometimes catches) the food himself. He is happy to accommodate groups of people, but reservations must be made at least a day in advance. Try the conch fritters and shark hash, but bring your own beer or liquor, as none is served here.

From the beach, follow Cashew City Road southeast past some old timber-frame homes. In a quarter of a mile you'll see the old pilot station, which has been converted into a school. Take a right just past it onto Great Bay Road; if you follow the shoreline you'll see locally made fishing boats rock in the harbor. Continue for just over a quarter of a mile until you see a path near *St. Luke's Church* that climbs up Lighthouse Hill. During the 17th century, the hill on which the lighthouse now stands was known as Stacey's Watch, probably after the settler who manned the station at that time. Make your way to *St. David's Lighthouse* at the top—it should take 10 minutes or so—and then climb the 85 steps to the balcony and take in the breathtaking views of Smith's Island directly to the northwest, St. George's to the north, and the US Naval Air Station to the west and south. Directly below the lighthouse is the spot where the yachts in the biennial *Newport–Bermuda Ocean Yacht Race* skim across the finish line. The lighthouse, which is built from Bermuda limestone quarried from the site, opened in 1879. It can be toured from May through September.

If you're ready for a break, stop in at the *New Mount Area* bar and restaurant just below the lighthouse (phone: 293-9783). To return home, retrace your route past St. Luke's or follow the longer route down the opposite side of the hill, taking Mount Road for a quarter of a mile, then turning left onto Luke's Lane, and then right on Texas Road. At the bottom of Texas Road, take a left and walk for 200 yards just past the post office to the *Black Horse Tavern,* an inexpensive seafood restaurant (see *Eating Out* in THE ISLAND). To return to the spot where you began, take a right onto Great Bay Road and walk a half mile back to the Great Head car park.

TUCKER'S TOWN

For a peek at one of Bermuda's toniest residential neighborhoods, climb onto your bike or moped and ride over to Tucker's Town. This exclusive neighborhood is located on the southeastern end of the main island of Bermuda, and it's bordered to the north and west by Hamilton Parish. The settlement is named for Governor Daniel Tucker, who planned to move the capital from St. George's to this site. In 1616, plans were drawn up, roads were built, and a couple of buildings went up before the idea was abandoned for lack of funds.

To get there, ride east from Smith's Parish along South Road. You'll pass the *Pink Beach Club,* the *Marsden Methodist Church,* and just after the road bends sharply to the right, Mangrove Lake. There are several turn-of-the-century homes just before you reach the *Mid Ocean Golf Club*—look out for flying golf balls! Continue east until you pass under a footbridge. You'll see Mid Ocean Drive on the right; about 150 yards beyond it, take the unmarked road that branches off to the right. Follow it for about a quarter of a mile past the club's tennis courts; across the street from them is *Overboard,* a grand old house built in the mid-19th century. Just beyond lies the private beach of Tucker's Town Bay, where many expensive small motorboats and yachts are moored. (A guard may bar you from riding east on Tucker's Town Road, which is private.)

Just across the water, at the mouth of the bay, is *Stokes Bay,* a lovely white house with blue shutters and several shady porches. If you like, take a detour to visit the Natural Arches (see *Natural Wonderlands* in DIVERSIONS) at the private beach of the *Mid Ocean Club* and *Marriott's Castle Harbour* hotel. From here, head northeast on Harrington Sound Road, which will take you to the *Idwal Hughes Nature Reserve* (see *Natural Wonderlands* in DIVERSIONS).

FERRY POINT PARK

Traveling by moped or bike is also the best way to see *Ferry Point Park.* About 5 miles west of the Olde Towne, it's the site of the strategically located Martello tower (see *Touring Bermuda's Forts* in DIVERSIONS). Open daily; no admission charge (no phone). On the way, watch out for dogs that guard the houses along Ferry Road. Don't be put off by them, though; it's a pleasant tour, and the park is a great place to explore on foot. The old railway line cuts through the southwestern edge of the park and leads to the northern tip of St. George's Island; you can follow this walking trail on your bike, but mopeds aren't allowed.

To start, take York Street west out of the Olde Towne; continue on until the road becomes Wellington Street and then Mullet Bay Road. You'll pass mangrove-fringed Mullet Bay on the left. After 2 miles, take the right fork onto Ferry Road. After a quarter of a mile or so you'll see the *Bermuda Biological Station for Research,* where marine biologists and environmental scientists work closely with the *National Science Foundation* and *Wood's Hole Oceanographic Institute* in Massachusetts. Some of its researchers are investigating the role that oceans may play in the greenhouse effect. Free tours are offered on Wednesdays at 10 AM (phone: 297-1880).

Follow the winding road for a mile and a half. You'll see Rogue and Little Rogue Islands and a bay called Ferry Reach before you reach the entrance to *Ferry Point Park.* The road dead-ends near a beach shaded by Australian pines. You can see the concrete plinths that once supported the railway trestle to Coney Island just to the west. Walk or bike down the railway trail along the northern coast, passing Lover's Lake, a natural catchment surrounded by mangroves and cactuses, on your right. Near the end of the trail stand the docks where tankers unload fuel for the island. It's best to backtrack along the railroad trail to the park, as you may run into dogs if you return via Anchorage View Lane.

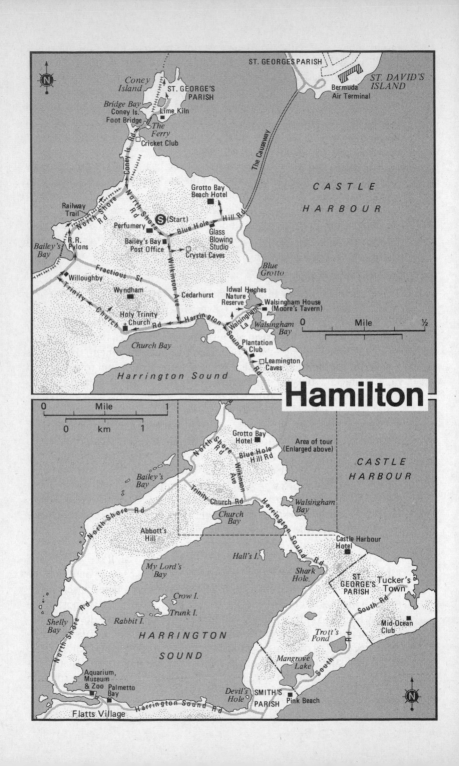

Hamilton

Hiking through Hamilton

Bordered by Harrington Sound, the north shore, and Castle Harbour, Hamilton Parish is pleasantly rural; there are limestone caves and cliffs to explore, as well as old inns and historic churches. Its gently hilly terrain can be negotiated on foot or on a bike or moped. Few roads have shoulders, however, and midday traffic can be heavy on Wilkinson Avenue and Harrington Sound Road, the two main thoroughfares leading to the airport. One way to avoid the midday rush is to stop at an inn for lunch or pack a picnic basket and head for the *Idwal Hughes Nature Reserve*.

Start this 4-mile walk at the 60-year-old *Bermuda Perfumery* (North Shore Rd.; phone: 293-0627; closed Sundays during winter). Before setting out, walk through its garden or tour the factory to find out how lilies, frangipani, passionflowers, and jasmine are pressed to make perfume. While the perfumery tends to be a bit commercial, the garden—with its impressive variety of aromatic trees and shrubs—is worth visiting. If you'd like a snack, turn right out of the parking lot and walk down about 100 yards to the intersection with Blue Hole Hill Road. On the left is the *Swizzle Inn* (phone: 293-9300), whose rum swizzles have gained the enthusiastic appreciation of visitors. Its walls and ceilings are plastered with business cards of a worldwide clientele; you might want to add your own to the collection. Try some delicious fish and chips with your drink. Afterward, don't deny yourself the treat of dessert across the street at *Bailey's Ice Cream Parlour* (see *Eating Out* in THE ISLAND). Thus fortified, walk down Blue Hill Road a quarter of a mile to the *Glass Blowing Studio* (phone: 293-2234), where demonstrations are held daily. Hour-long workshops are held several mornings a week. Across the street is the *Grotto Bay Beach* hotel, which has cork-surface tennis courts and boats for hire.

Return to the intersection of North Shore and Blue Hill Roads. At Bailey's Bay Post Office, turn onto Wilkinson Avenue; one door down is *The Bungalow,* an 18th-century home with a wide verandah facing the road. Just past the house on the left is the entrance to *Crystal Caves.* Discovered in 1908 by a boy who was looking for his lost ball, the caves are part of an ancient network of natural formations under Castle Harbour. An attraction for spelunkers and landlubbers (except claustrophobic ones) alike, the caves are worth a visit. Since they were discovered relatively recently, the caves escaped damage from the pre-electricity–age practice of burning palmetto leaves for illumination, a practice that marred many of Bermuda's beautiful caverns. The stalactites and stalagmites remain a lovely pale beige and white (also see *Natural Wonderlands* in DIVERSIONS). The caves are closed in December and January; open daily the rest of the year; admission charge (phone: 293-0640). A branch of the *Bermuda Railway Company,* which sells sportswear, is located just to the right of the exit from the caves.

Continue down Wilkinson Avenue past the Mormon church and *Cedarhurst,* a white colonial home surrounded by date palms. From here you can look out over Harrington Sound to Hall's Island. Near the shore is the junction of Harrington Sound and Trinity Church Roads. Here you have a choice: You can take a left onto Harrington Sound Road, which leads to the *Idwal Hughes Nature Reserve,* or you can turn right onto Trinity Church Road, which will take you on a mile-long loop back to the *Bermuda Perfumery* via North Shore Road.

If you choose the first route, you'll round several bends on Harrington Sound Road, which has a fair volume of traffic, until you see Walsingham Lane on the left. Walk down this quiet lane, which is bordered with high hedges of Bermuda cherry, until you see a sign on the left for the *Idwal Hughes Nature Reserve* (see *Natural Wonderlands* in DIVERSIONS), which is part of the *Walsingham Trust* property. The park is open daily; no admission charge (no phone).

The trail through the reserve leads back to Walsingham Lane; proceed down it to the white house at the end. This is *Walsingham House,* which was built in 1652 by Nicholas Trott, an officer of the Bermuda Company. Irish lawyer and poet Tom Moore visited here frequently in the early 1800s and is said to have written many poems under a nearby calabash tree. *Walsingham House*—the first home in Bermuda to be formally named—is now the home of the elegant *Tom Moore's Tavern* (see *Eating Out* in THE ISLAND).

If you retrace your steps to Harrington Sound Road and continue south, you will pass the driveway to a house called *Clisdell;* just beyond it is a yellow and white house called the *Plantation,* which serves a diverse menu of continental and Bermudian dishes at lunch and dinner (see *Eating Out* in THE ISLAND). *Leamington Caves,* a small network of limestone grottoes with amber-colored stalagmites, are located just south of the house (also see *Natural Wonderlands* in DIVERSIONS). Open daily; admission charge (no phone). The bus stops here, or you can return home by cab.

If you choose the alternate route that takes you down Trinity Church Road, you'll soon pass a whitewashed 17th-century house with several chimneys and a gabled slate roof. Continue down this quiet residential street for just over a quarter of a mile to *Holy Trinity Church* and its graveyard, which overlooks Harrington Sound. Well worth a stop, it's one of the most serene spots in the island. Note the stone mounting steps in the yard, where churchgoers would alight from their horses.

Just past the church is the entrance to *Mount Wyndham,* a private house on the right. The road climbs steadily here, and if you glance behind you'll have an impressive view of Harrington Sound. Surinam cherries and palmettos line the route. Take a right onto North Shore Road and head downhill to Bailey's Bay (notice the pylons that once supported the railway trestle that crossed the bay). You'll pass *Willoughby,* an 18th-century home on the right. Owned in 1794 by the Hon. Samuel Trott, also the owner of

Walsingham House, it originally consisted of four rooms with outbuildings and a buttery; the house was extended to its present state during the 19th century. There is a small beach just beyond and across from it, but it's not an ideal place to swim, for the traffic noise can be annoying. Just past the beach is a turnoff to the left that leads to the railway trail. You can call a cab from the phone there, or walk down the trail for half a mile or so; there are high limestone cliffs on the left, and you'll have an occasional glimpse of the ocean. Unfortunately, you can't continue far on the trail, for several bridges that once spanned gaps in the rocky shoreline have crumbled, and it's difficult to scramble up and down the boulders. Eventually the railway trail will bend to the right, and you'll see Coney Island Road branch off to your left; bear right, and in a quarter mile or so the trail intersects with North Shore Road; follow North Shore Road east and you'll soon be back at the perfumery.

If you like, continue roughly northeast down Coney Island Road and cross the bridge to Coney Island, which predates the beach/amusement park area in Brooklyn, New York. A small footbridge—said to be Bermuda's first bridge—was the only link connecting Bermuda's Coney Island (which appeared as "Cony" on Norwood's earliest survey map) to the main island and St. George's. From this vantage point, there's a fine view of the Martello tower just across the channel on St. George's Island (see *Touring Bermuda's Forts* in DIVERSIONS). You can also explore the ruins of an old lime kiln here, but be forewarned: This is a favorite spot for motorbikers, so it's hardly the tranquil haven that you might expect.

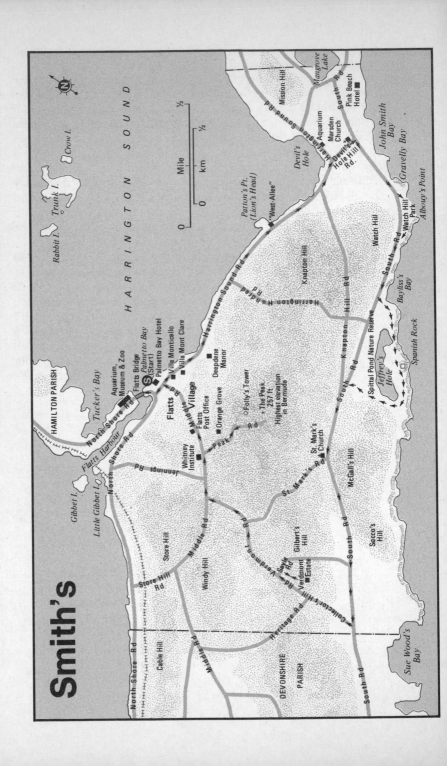

Sauntering in Smith's

It's hard to believe that parts of serene Smith's Parish were once havens for smugglers. Much more credible—and more enduring—are its wealth of marine life, its caves, its historic homes, and its spectacular views.

Both bicyclists and walkers can use the following two routes through the parish; moped riders can as well, though they'll need to make a detour around the trail at Spittal Pond. The first route, which covers about 7 miles, starts from Flatts Village, skirts the south shore of Harrington Sound to the nature reserve at Spittal Pond, and ends at *Verdmont*, one of Bermuda's best-preserved historic homes. The second route, which is only 2 miles long, starts at *Verdmont* and takes a direct downhill route to Flatts Village.

To make the 7-mile circuit, take a bus or taxi to Flatts Village and get off at the *Palmetto* hotel. Founded in the 17th century, Flatts Village was favored by sea captains and smugglers, for its bay is calm and sheltered. Walk through the hotel grounds, which are shaded by an enormous mahogany tree, until you reach Harrington Sound Road, then take a left. Around the first bend is *Villa Monticello,* a brown 17th-century home, and *Villa Mont Clare,* a 19th-century mansion surrounded by a two-tiered verandah with delicately carved railings. You'll walk under a footbridge that once linked guests of the *Deepdene Manor* to a private beach; what remains of the manor has been turned into condominiums.

For the next 2 miles or so, the road runs parallel to the shoreline; you can see snappers and sergeant majors swimming in the clear water. You'll pass *Sargasso Cottage,* a beige house with blue shutters just at the water's edge on the left; across the bay three private isles are visible, the largest of which is Trunk Island. About a mile and a half east of Flatts Village, just past Harrington Hundred Road, is a slender finger of land covered with Australian pines; just past it at the water's edge is *West-Alee,* a home that has been beautifully restored after being destroyed by waves in a 1987 hurricane. On the right, past Knapton Hill, there is a brick-colored 17th-century home with a large limestone chimney and a gabled slate roof; these features, and its "welcoming arms" entrance, are typical of Bermuda's early colonial houses.

About 100 feet farther down on the right is the entrance to *Devil's Hole Aquarium,* where you can indulge in a curious sport. Sea turtles, gray sharks, groupers, and hogfish swim in a large pond edged with coral; by holding a bit of bait tied to a line—no rods or hooks allowed—you can lure the fish to you, and if you can pull one up you get to keep it. (The fish are wily, so your chances aren't good.) During the early 19th century the deep pool was used as a storage pond to keep fish until they were ready to be cooked. When its owner, a Mr. Trott, tired of local fishermen helping themselves to his stock, he built a wall around the pool. Before long the enterprising

Trott was charging an entrance fee to those who wanted to look inside the walls. Open daily; admission charge (phone: 293-2072).

Take a right just after the aquarium and head up the gentle incline of Devil's Hole Hill for a few hundred yards. Turn right onto South Road and continue bearing right along the shore to John Smith's Bay. The pink and white sand here is clean and fine, and the water is calm and shallow. This is a good place to swim or scuba dive—bring your own equipment, for there is none for rent here. Snorkelers should explore Gravelly Bay just to the southwest, where they'll see damselfish, doctorfish, and sergeant majors.

You'll skirt this bay as you continue walking along South Road; a quarter mile beyond it is a promontory called Albuoy's Point. Make your way along the stony path at the water's edge—if you're cycling, leave your bike and walk this stretch—and look for parrot fish and doctorfish darting to and fro in the deep water. (Watch out for holes along the trail; they're dug by land crabs.) The trail soon joins up again with South Road, and you'll pass a grassy spot called Watch Hill Park; beyond it the road is bordered by stone walls. To the left, cliffs drop 30 feet into the sea.

Half a mile past Albuoy's Point is a sign marking the footpath that leads to *Spittal Pond Nature Reserve.* This 50-acre sanctuary—the island's largest—is home to perhaps 200 species of native and migratory birds, including dotterels, North American warblers, house martins, terns, cardinals, and eastern bluebirds. Hikers are advised not to deviate from the trails that meander through the woods and marshlands; the habitats of the birds are fragile, and it's best not to crash straight through them. A few hundred yards down, the trail divides; take the right-hand fork, which skirts the eastern edge of the pond. In a quarter of a mile there's another fork. Take the left-hand path, which leads to the misnamed Spanish Rock, where a shipwrecked Portuguese sailor—one of the first known visitors to Bermuda—clambered ashore in 1543. (The rock has been coated with bronze to protect it from vandals.) Jeffrey's Hole, a cave named for a runaway slave who took refuge here more than a century ago, is entered through an opening at the top of the cliff. Continue west on the path for another quarter of a mile. If you're lucky, you may see a blue heron or hear the three-note call of the yellow-breasted kiskadee. If you'd like to learn more about the wildlife in the area, contact the *Department of Agriculture* (phone: 236-4201), which offers guided tours of the refuge. *Spittal Pond Nature Reserve* is open daily; no admission charge (no phone). Also see *Natural Wonderlands* in DIVERSIONS.

The last leg of the trail dips and climbs through pastureland until it reaches the parking lot at the western edge of the refuge. From there, take a left onto South Road and walk several hundred feet, past the junction with Knapton Hill Road. Bear left and climb steadily for half a mile or so; you'll soon see the limestone spire of *St. Mark's Church,* built during the 19th century in Gothic style. It stands near the site of the original 17th-century parish church, which was destroyed long ago. Walk around the church and admire its English stained glass windows. Note the limestone tombs in the graveyard, which resemble those found in parts of Louisiana; each family owns a vault, and the dead are buried in cedar caskets. The church, its graveyard, and the *Church Hall* are worth a leisurely tour. There's a phone in the parking lot if you'd like to call a cab, and buses stop on both sides of the street.

If your energy hasn't flagged, take a right out of the church parking lot and walk down the steep hill to South Road, then make another right. In half a mile or so is *Verdmont,* a beautifully preserved early-18th-century mansion, which is open to the public. If you like, enter the property by a more roundabout route by continuing down South Road. In just over a mile you'll come to the *Cottage Bakery* (phone: 236-0269), where you can enjoy afternoon tea or pick up an entire box lunch, ice cream, or just an eclair. Past the bakery, make a sharp right onto Collector's Hill Road (so named because the tax collector lived here in the 19th century). Near the crest of the hill, make a right onto Sayle Road. The entrance to *Verdmont* is about 10 feet down on the right. The house is closed Sundays; admission charge (see *Historic Homes and Gardens* in DIVERSIONS). After you've seen the house, call a cab or walk back down Collector's Hill to catch a bus in either direction.

The 2-mile route from *Verdmont* back to Flatts Village leads past some historic homes, old limestone walls, and forests filled with cedars, fiddlewoods, and cherries. Leaving from the north entrance to *Verdmont,* turn right onto Verdmont Road (which is called Collector's Hill in the opposite direction). Follow this quiet lane, which is bordered by stone walls; it veers sharply to the right just beyond Gilbert Hill, and from there the road passes through banana patches and potato fields. For the next three-quarters of a mile or so along the roadside are stumps from cedar trees destroyed by the blight that swept through Bermuda in the 1940s. At the intersection with Middle Road, there's a grocery store where you can pick up a snack; from the store, take a right onto Middle Road and continue past Jennings Road, where there was once a golf course, and the *Whitney Institute,* a primary and secondary school. Just opposite the school is Peak Road, which leads to the highest spot in Bermuda—a hill 259 feet above sea level–hardly a "peak" in any other place. The road is private, though, so continue on past *Calabash Cottage* and *Orange Grove* on the right and the parish post office on the left. From here there is a good view of Harrington Sound and the shores of Harrington Parish beyond it.

Walk down a short incline and bear left to a row of coconut palms lining the blue-green water of the inlet. To the right is the *Palmetto* hotel, whose *Inlet* restaurant serves a variety of good local fish dishes; if you're here September through March, be sure to sample their stuffed spiny lobster. Rack of lamb and steaks are also on the menu. Or take a left and walk past the row of gumdrop-colored houses to the *Halfway House* bar and grill. (For more details on both restaurants, see *Eating Out* in THE ISLAND.) Across the bay, on the other side of the bridge, is the *Bermuda Aquarium, Museum and Zoo,* where you can see everything from sharks and moray eels to Galápagos tortoises and cockatoos; there is also a small natural history museum. Both are open daily; admission charge (phone: 293-2727). From here you can call a cab or take a bus or ferry to take you back to your Bermuda home.

Dawdling in Devonshire

Though it's only a short distance from the capital, Devonshire has managed to retain a good deal of its rural character. There are still many working farms nestled in small valleys, and even tracts of unspoiled forest remain. There is a large private nature reserve here, one of the island's best golf courses, and a fine 17th-century church.

The first two routes described here cover about 5 miles, and follow quiet roadways and part of the old railway bed. Both follow Parson's Lane and the Orange Valley and North Shore Roads; the first route is better for bicycles, as it follows the railway trail for only a quarter of a mile. The third route, which is half a mile longer than the first two, leads to *Palm Grove,* one of the island's loveliest estates, and the *Devonshire Bay Battery.*

WESTERN DEVONSHIRE

The first route begins at the Devonshire Post Office on Orange Valley Road near the intersection with Middle Road. If you look down the left-hand side of Middle Road from the post office, you'll spy one of the island's few remaining wooden houses; decorated with gingerbread trim and painted a prim white, it stands just to the east of *Sunnylands,* a private home. Walk three-quarters of a mile down Orange Valley Road, past *Devonshire Marsh,* a 65-acre nature reserve owned by the government of Bermuda, the *Bermuda National Trust,* and the *Bermuda Audubon Society.* There are several lovely estates just past the reserve, including *The Grove,* which sits on land once owned by Gideon Delawne, apothecary to Queen Elizabeth I, and *Orange Valley,* whose 15-acre grounds are shaded by cedars, mahoganies, black ebonies, and poincianas.

At the end of the road, take a left onto Parson's Lane, which is bordered by Surinam cherry trees (Bermudians make jams and jellies from their sweet fruit). Continue up the hill for half a mile or so to Palmetto Road, then take a right. In 1903, the grounds here were headquarters for members of the British military stationed in Bermuda. Offering one of the best views on the island, the former Garrison Officers' Mess lawn is fanned by cool breezes from the ocean even in the heat of summer. The British must have liked to keep their men happy: The nearby *Ocean View* golf course was built for members of the garrison. You can see the *Royal Naval Dockyard* and the eastern parishes from this vantage point. There are benches here where visitors can sit and take in the views of the ocean and the coastline. (All along these walks are benches or grassy knolls where you can pause to eat a snack—or just to fully enjoy the surroundings.)

Less than half a mile farther on is a sign on the right for the railway trail; it's located just where Palmetto Road curves to the left before it descends

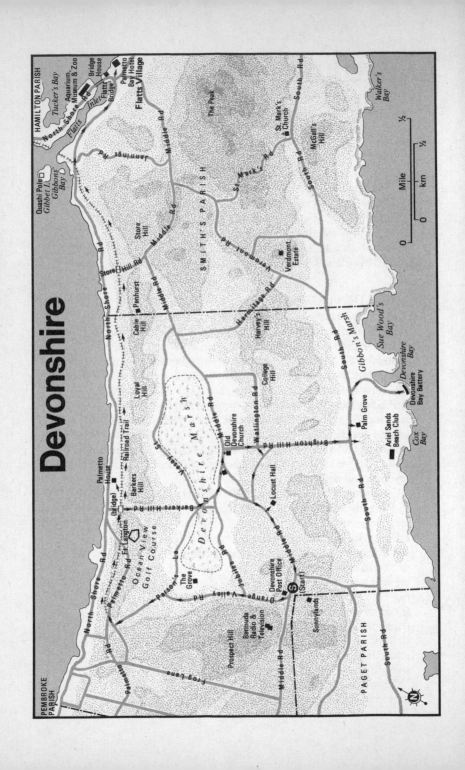

Devonshire

HAMILTON PARISH

Quashi Pole
Gibbet I.
Gibbons Bay

Tucker's Bay

North Shore Rd

Flatts Inlet

Flatts Bridge

Aquarium, Museum & Zoo

Bridge House

Palmetto Bay Hotel

Flatts Village

Walker's Bay

The Peak

St. Mark's Church

South Rd

McGall's Hill

Jennings Rd

Middle Rd

S M I T H ' S   P A R I S H

St. Mark's Rd

South Rd

Store Hill

Store Hill Rd

Middle Rd

Penhurst

Verdmont Estate

North Shore Rd

Cable Hill

Middle Rd

Hermitage Rd

Harvey's Hill

Sue Wood's Bay

Devonshire Bay

Loyal Hill

Railroad Trail

St. Rd

College Hill

Wallington Rd

South Rd

Gibbon's Marsh

Devonshire Bay Battery

Palmetto House

Barkers Hill

D e v o n s h i r e   M a r s h

Middle Rd

Old Devonshire Church

Brighton Hill Rd

Palm Grove

Ariel Sands Beach Club

Cox Bay

(bridge)

Barkers Hill Rd

Fort Langton

Ocean View Golf Course

Parson's La.

The Grove

Locust Hall

Middle Rd

South Rd

North Shore Rd

Palmetto Rd

Orange Valley Rd

Devonshire Post Office

(Start)

Sunnylands

Bermuda Radio & Television

Prospect Hill

Frog Lane

Middle Rd

PEMBROKE PARISH

PAGET PARISH

South Rd

Mile

km

½   ½

0

N

to North Shore Road. Take this trail and in a quarter of a mile you'll cross the old railway bridge at Barkers Hill. Just beyond the bridge on the left is *Palmetto House,* which is open to visitors on Thursdays; no admission charge (see *Historic Homes and Gardens* in DIVERSIONS). To the right is the 9-hole, government-operated *Ocean View* golf course (phone: 236-6737). At this point, you can retrace your steps back to Barkers Hill Road or walk to the town of Flatts Village in Smith's Parish; the second option will be described in our second route.

It's a steep half-mile climb up Barkers Hill, and it only takes a look back to see the turquoise waters of the Atlantic along the north shore. At the crest of the hill, walk down the sharp incline to the intersection of Vesey Street and Parsons Lane. Turn left onto Parsons Lane and continue for a quarter of a mile to Middle Road. Along this stretch the road cuts through the lush vegetation of Devonshire Marsh. After crossing Middle Road— watch for traffic, as it's one of the island's busiest thoroughfares—walk a few hundred yards to the simple whitewashed 17th-century *Old Devonshire Church.* Note that there are two churches here: the new church, where there are regular services and a special candlelight service just before *Christmas,* and the smaller, more historic old church, which was rebuilt to its original specifications, following an explosion in 1970. Wander through the graveyard and peer in through the church windows.

Leave the churchyard through the side gate that opens onto Brighton Hill Road, then take a right and climb the steep hill to the junction with Watlington Road East, where you'll find *Lindo's Market* (phone: 236-5623), a good place to pick up light provisions. Take the little lane that branches off to the right from Brighton Hill Road, just across from the store, to Watlington Road West. Walk down this road for half a mile; there are truck gardens to the left and the Saltus Cavendish Preparatory School on the right. Take a left onto Middle Road; about 30 feet farther, on the left, is the entrance to *Locust Hall,* an 18th-century house surrounded by 24 acres of farmland. The *Bermuda National Trust* (phone: 236-6483) is building a network of trails through the property, but it's still unfinished, so it's best to call to find out what you can—and cannot—explore. To return, continue down Middle Road for half a mile, until you see Orange Valley Road on your right; you also can catch a bus at one of several stops along the way.

RAILROAD TRAIL

Our second suggested route leads along the railway path for just under 3 miles, from Barkers Hill to Flatts Village. After you pass *Palmetto House,* walk about three-quarters of a mile, crossing Loyal Hill Road, until you reach the *Clay House Inn,* which overlooks the water; it's one of the island's best nightclubs (see *Nightclubs and Nightlife* in THE ISLAND). In another quarter of a mile, just beyond Cable Hill, you'll cross the border into Smith's Parish.

The origin of Flatts Village is obscure. Some claim it was so named because of the shallow water here, but records show that oceangoing ships managed to anchor in the harbor here during the 17th century. During its heyday, Flatts Village held a position of prominence second only to St. George's. In 1761, the Assembly convened here when the capital was threatened by invasion by French privateers. Flatts Bridge is said to have been the first to be built in the colony. In 1620, when the first Assembly authorized the construction of footbridges at Somerset and Coney Island, it decreed that ". . . the bridge which is already erected at the fflatts ouer [sic] of the little sound be made more substantial." The drawbridge was raised for passing ships; the bridgekeeper lived in (where else?) *Bridge House,* a 17th-century home on Harrington Sound, just east of the bridge.

A few hundred yards away from the parish line, the land is part of *Penhurst Park;* you can walk down to the dock to your left and take a swim. Just beyond the park, cross the bridge over Store Hill Road and traverse some beautiful properties, including *Millwood* on the right. You'll be walking parallel to North Shore Road, but the track is elevated along this stretch and the views are spectacular. The trail then curves northeast and runs into North Shore Road; cross the road (look to your right) and pick up the trail on the other side. You'll soon see sandy-bottomed Gibbons Bay and Gibbet and Little Gibbet islands, just at the mouth of Flatts Inlet. You can't swim here, though—all the beaches are private. During the 17th century, Gibbet Island was used as a place of public execution; at least two men were hanged here. The remains of the gibbet used for a hanging in 1754 was named Quashi's Pole, after a convicted slave who met his own death in similar fashion.

The trail leads to within 100 yards of the beaches, on the south side of the Flatts Inlet. Coconut palms line the shore on the opposite side of the channel, and there's a yellow 19th-century house across the bay. In another quarter of a mile you'll enter Flatts Village, one of the most picturesque towns on the island. The bay here is sheltered, with many wooden fishing boats moored safely. Follow North Shore Road into town; you'll pass several 18th-century buildings wedged between the water and the road. Across the street is the *Halfway House* bar and grill, and about 300 yards farther is the *Palmetto* hotel, which serves good grilled fish in its *Inlet* restaurant (see *Eating Out* in THE ISLAND for details on both restaurants). The *Bermuda Aquarium, Museum and Zoo* is just on the other side of the bridge across the bay. If you're vacationing with children, be sure to stop by for a visit (for details see *Sauntering in Smith's,* in this section).

PALM GROVE AND DEVONSHIRE BAY BATTERY

To reach *Palm Grove,* with its moongate and its grass "map" of Bermuda, and the ruins of the *Devonshire Bay Battery,* turn right onto Brighton Hill Road from the *Old Devonshire* churchyard and follow the road, which is lined with old stone walls and cherry trees, for a quarter of a mile up a slight rise until it descends to South Road. The entrance to *Palm Grove* is on the left (for details, see *Historic Homes and Gardens* in DIVERSIONS). Closed Fridays through Sundays; no admission charge (phone: 236-8144). Next to the entrance is the *Ariel Sands Beach Club;* the colony of cottages is named for the sprite in Shakespeare's *The Tempest,* which is supposedly set in Bermuda. The restaurant here serves excellent red bean soup. Continue on Brighton Hill Road, take a left onto South Road, and then walk down half a mile; Devonshire Bay Road is on the right. Take this road; it curves to the right along a protected harbor and leads straightaway to the *Devonshire Bay Battery* (see *Touring Bermuda's Forts* in DIVERSIONS). The fort is open daily; no admission charge (no phone).

ON TWO WHEELS

You can cycle along all of three of our walking routes, but if you want to see the bridge at Barkers Hill, it's best to head down Palmetto Road to North Shore Road and take a right up the paved street. To see *Palmetto House,* continue past Barkers Hill for a few hundred yards; it's on the right.

Moped riders can follow the same routes, with only a few detours. Since mopeds aren't allowed on the railway trail, riders must head down Palmetto Road to North Shore Road, follow the traffic circle around to the right, and then head south up Barkers Hill Road to pick up the first walking route. Moped riders can also visit *Palm Grove* and the *Devonshire Bay Battery* by following the walking trail from Brighton Hill Road. You can also ride to Flatts Village, which is about 2½ miles from the traffic circle where Palmetto and North Shore Roads meet. *Palmetto House* is just a few hundred feet from this junction, past Barkers Hill Road.

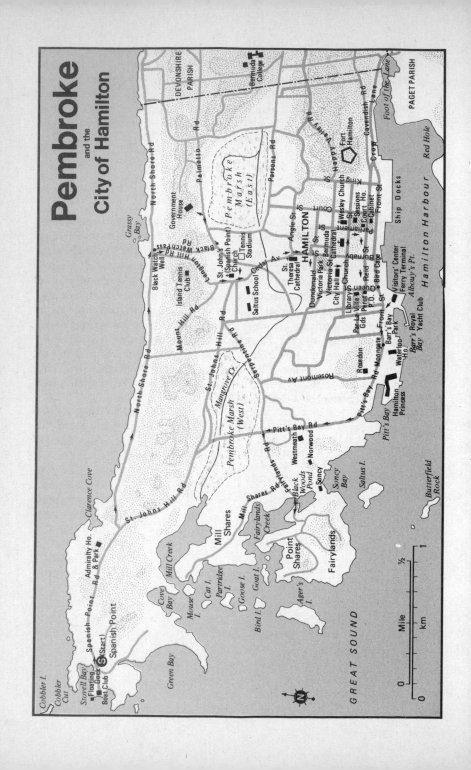

Passing through Pembroke and the City of Hamilton

It may not be true that William Shakespeare wrote *The Tempest* somewhere in a cavern in Bermuda—as some local taxi drivers would have you believe—but it *is* true that the parish of Pembroke is named for one of the playwright's friends and patrons, William Herbert, the third Earl of Pembroke. (Shakespeare dedicated the first folio printing of his collected works to him.) This parish, located on a peninsula in central Bermuda, is the most populous on the island. Hamilton, the capital, stands on a sheltered harbor in southern Pembroke, and one of the colony's most impressive forts guards the hill overlooking the city. Although it is densely settled, it's still possible to find many secluded spots to explore. Walk or cycle along the two routes described here, which lead to most of the loveliest spots in the parish.

SPANISH POINT TO DOWNTOWN HAMILTON

Our first tour, which covers about 5 miles, runs past the home of the Governor of Bermuda, some handsome residential neighborhoods, and the historic district in downtown Hamilton. Start by taking a bus to *Spanish Point Park,* on the western edge of Pembroke. It was here, in 1603, that the Spanish captain Diego Ramírez wrecked his galleon on a reef. It's said that an early explorer erected a large wooden cross here. The cross, according to local lore, was inscribed with directions to a pool of fresh water. Settlers who came across the landmark later were in for a disappointment, for they thought it pointed the way to buried treasure.

Just west of the entrance to the park is Stovell Bay, a secluded area that's worth a detour. At the mouth of the bay is the wreckage of a floating dock that broke away as it was being towed across the harbor in 1904. Hike down to the picturesque coves north of the bay. It's a good place to swim, for the surf is gentle here, and there are lots of pretty shells on the sand. During the summer and fall, there are often one or more gaily decorated cruise ships that can be glimpsed sailing out of the channel on their way back to New York. (You'll find a phone and changing rooms near the park's entrance, and you can buy snacks from a stand here during the summer.)

Continue east up Spanish Point Road for three-quarters of a mile or so to *Admiralty Park;* it's a gentle climb the whole way. You'll pass several small roads, including Old House, Sugar Apple, and Seagull Lanes, and a turn-of-the-century tan-and-white homestead called *Highland Villa.* Just before getting to the park, there's a green clapboard house surrounded by cedars; it's one of the few remaining wooden homes on the island.

Admiralty Park is named for the British admirals who lived here in fine style during the 19th century, when the operations at the *Royal Naval Dockyard* (also known as simply the *Dockyard*) just across the sound on Ireland Island North, were in full swing. (A private ferry took the admiral and his retinue back and forth to the *Dockyard* each day.) The admiral's home was demolished several years ago, but the ballroom, which is decorated with gingerbread trim, is still visible, and if you stroll around the grounds you can stand under some towering cedars and palms planted by British royalty more than a century ago.

After walking through the park, visit Clarence Cove, one of the best beaches on Bermuda's north coast. To get there, take the winding concrete path lined with cedars and palmettos just to the right of the parking lot (the path's surface was corrugated so that naval officers, shod in smooth-soled leather boots, wouldn't slip while marching to the dock). Longtails nest in the cliffs that rise above the cove, and the shore is pocked with caves that snorkelers can explore. Many Bermudian scuba divers train here. If you stand on the dock you can look across the sound to the twin towers of the *Dockyard,* almost 2 miles away.

Turn left out of the main gate and walk about 100 yards to North Shore Road, then take another left. *St. John's Hill House,* a graceful 18th-century home, is just across the way. Walk just under 2 miles to the junction of Black Watch Pass and Langton Hill Road, taking a break now and then to watch the waves break along the rocky shore. Left of the junction is a grassy knoll where a 17th-century ducking stool once stood. (It's been moved to the town of St. George's.) To the right is the *Black Watch Well,* which was dug by soldiers from the 42nd division of the Royal Scottish Highlanders during the drought of 1849. Turn right onto Black Watch Pass, which cuts through a massive outcropping of limestone; another right turn leads to the excellent public courts at the *Government Tennis Stadium* (for details, see *Choice Courts* in THE ISLAND).

To continue on to Hamilton, climb up Langton Hill Road past the gates of the *Government House,* a Victorian mansion where the Governor of Bermuda lives. You can just glimpse the house through the groves of Australian pine. (It was there, in 1973, that Governor Richard Sharples and an aide were assassinated—one of the few violent incidents in modern Bermudian history.) For a panoramic view of the capital, take a detour up Robin Hood Drive. If you continue on Langton Hill Road you'll soon reach *St. John's,* the parish church. Originally called *Spanish Point Church,* it was built in 1621. Forge up the hill past *Saltus Grammar School* and round the bend to Cedar Avenue, then make a right turn. In half a mile or so, this will bring you to downtown Hamilton.

The city of Hamilton was founded in 1790, more than 175 years after the town of St. George's, and parishioners in western Bermuda paid their customs duties here. It remained a sleepy backwater until 1815, when the governor and the House of Assembly moved their offices here.

Halfway down Cedar Avenue on the right is the tall Italianate tower of *St. Theresa's Roman Catholic Cathedral,* which was completed in 1932. A few blocks farther down is *Victoria Park* (see *Historic Homes and Gardens* in DIVERSIONS). Open daily; no admission charge for children under 12. Walk south through this prim little park, past the silver gazebo in the center, which was built in the 1880s to commemorate the *Golden Jubilee* of Queen Victoria's reign. If you're lucky, you may hear the strains of martial music, for bands play here now and then.

Cross Victoria Street and walk up Washington Street, a narrow lane that leads to Church Street. To the right is the tall white tower of *City Hall,* which is modeled after the municipal building in Stockholm. A weathervane bearing a replica of the *Sea Venture*—the English ship that was wrecked on a reef off St. George's in 1609—is perched on top. Turn left onto Church Street to see the *Cathedral of the Most Holy Trinity,* built in the English Gothic style and consecrated in 1911; rest for a bit in one of the carved cedar pews and admire the Angel Window on the east wall, which was designed by a local artist. When you've revived, continue east to Parliament Street; you'll find the island's main post office on the southwest corner.

Just across from the post office is the *Sessions House,* which opened in 1817. Its clock tower and terra cotta Florentine façade were added in 1887 to celebrate Queen Victoria's *Golden Jubilee.* Bermuda's Parliament—the fourth-oldest in the world, after those of England, Iceland, and the Isle of Man—convenes here. You can watch a spirited debate in the House of Assembly on Fridays starting at 10 AM (during budget sessions, from late February to mid-March, it sits on Mondays and Wednesdays as well); the legislature is in session from late October or early November to late June or early July, with one-month breaks for *Christmas* and *Easter.* To reach the public gallery, walk through the entrance on Parliament Street and climb the flight of stairs. (Dress conservatively; those wearing jeans or miniskirts will be turned away.) Note the gavel wielded by the Speaker of the House; it is carved from a limb of the ancient cedar that stands in the courtyard of *St. Peter's Church* in St. George's, where Bermuda's first Parliament convened in 1620. If you would like to arrange a visit on another day during the week, contact the sergeant at arms (phone: 292-7408).

The Supreme Court meets downstairs in the south side of the *Sessions House.* (You can sit and listen if you like, unless a closed hearing is in session.) For an insider's view of the foibles of Bermudian society, you can also visit the plea court, located in the *Magistrate's Court* just south of the main gate of the *Sessions House* on the corner of Parliament and Reid

Streets. Here people accused of crimes state their guilt or innocence. The plea court convenes weekdays at 2:30 PM.

Across from the *Magistrate's Court* on Reid Street rises the severe neoclassical façade of the *Cabinet Building.* Constructed of native limestone between 1833 and 1836, it is one of Bermuda's most imposing public structures. Inside is a cedar throne carved in 1642; it is from here that the Governor of Bermuda delivers his address at the opening session of Parliament each fall. The Bermuda Senate—which, unlike the US Senate, wields far less power than the House–meets here at 10 AM on Wednesdays from November to June; you can sit in on a session if you like. Just across from the *Cabinet Building* on Front Street stands the *Cenotaph,* a memorial to the Bermudians who died in the two world wars. The Prince of Wales (later King Edward VIII, who abdicated to marry American socialite Wallis Warfield Simpson) laid the cornerstone for this monument in 1920. To the west is Front Street, what was once Hamilton's Savile Row. During the 1920s, the tailors who worked on this street launched the fashion craze for Bermuda shorts, which were adapted from the summer uniform worn by British soldiers (see *Quintessential Bermuda* in DIVERSIONS). The street is now occupied by many fine clothiers and haberdashers (see *Shopping* in THE ISLAND for details).

Walk down Front Street, along the water's edge, to Queen Street, 2 blocks west of Parliament Street. Just before the intersection is the so-called "birdcage," a covered pedestal where policemen directed traffic in the days before stoplights were installed (you may still see a bobby here at rush hour). The visitors' service bureau is half a block to the west, next to the ferry terminal (phone: 295-1480).

Just up Queen Street on the left is the Perot Post Office, which is housed in a simple whitewashed building. The island's first postmaster, William Bennett Perot, worked here from 1818 to 1862. During Perot's time, mail was carried from one parish to the other by ferry and horse-drawn coach; it cost a penny to send a letter from Hamilton to Somerset or St. George's. On the advice of his friend James Heyl, who ran an apothecary next door to the post office, Perot designed a 1-cent stamp that residents could buy by the sheet and glue onto their letters. In 1989, a Perot stamp fetched $240,000 at auction.

You can mail your own letters at the post office here and then relax on the verandah of the adjacent *Bermuda Library and Historical Society,* which was formerly the home of Perot and his wife and nine children. Perot himself planted the enormous rubber tree that shades the garden, which has been turned into a park (see "Par-la-Ville Gardens" in *Historic Homes and Gardens,* DIVERSIONS). The *Bermuda Historical Society Museum* is on the property, and there's also a library. The park is open daily; the library and museum are closed Sundays; no admission charge (phone: 295-2905, library; 295-2487, museum).

TO FAIRYLANDS AND POINT SHARES

Our second suggested route covers between 3 and 5 miles, depending on the number of side roads you decide to explore. It runs from the ferry terminal in Hamilton to Fairylands and Point Shares, two of the island's most exclusive residential neighborhoods. To avoid rush-hour traffic, it's best to set out after 9 AM and return before 4 PM. You could also hire a horse and buggy to drive you along this scenic route in the evening.

From the ferry stop, head west on Front Street, which later becomes Pitt's Bay Road. On the left is *Barr's Bay Park,* where there's a fine view of the pink buildings of the *Royal Bermuda Yacht Club* and the boats moored in Hamilton Harbour. Make a wish at the moongate a few hundred yards past the park next to the *Bermuda Bakery.* Across the street is *Waterloo House,* an inn with a cozy dining room. Stop by in the late afternoon; you can sip tea on the terrace and watch the sun go down over the harbor. A few hundred feet farther down on the right is Bacardi International, Ltd., the international headquarters for the rum distillery. Just past it on the right is the *Pegasus Print and Map Shop* (phone: 295-2900), the best place in Bermuda to buy antique maps.

Another hundred yards along the road is the *Hamilton Princess* hotel. Built in 1885, it's named for Princess Louise, a daughter of Queen Victoria, who vacationed in Bermuda during the winter of 1882–83. In the early decades of the 20th century, the hotel attracted a glittering social set. During World War II, the British government set up a censorship station here for mail bound from the US to Europe. Just around the corner from the hotel is Pitt's Bay, where many wealthy Bermudians moor their boats. Press on for a quarter of a mile to the crest of the hill; be sure to stop to look at the view of the harbor and Paget Parish to the south.

As you walk the next three-quarter-mile stretch to Fairylands Road, you'll pass many lovely homes, including *Old Walls, Netherby, Trelawny,* and *Norwood,* which was built by the granddaughter of Richard Norwood, who conducted the first survey of the island. *Norwood*'s cruciform plan was believed to ward off evil spirits. If your visit coincides with one of the *Garden Club of Bermuda*'s periodic tours of the property, you can lose yourself in the maze of neatly trimmed hedges in the garden. Note the famous sign posted here, which reads "Private Grounds: Where tramps *must* not, Surely ladies and gentlemen *will* not trespass." Turn left onto Fairylands Road and walk just under half a mile to Mill Shares Road, then take a right. Here are more hand-painted signs announcing the names of the houses; *Mayfair* and *The Palms* are two of the finest.

Just beyond the turnoff to Point Shares Road, on the left behind a hibiscus hedge, is *Soncy Cottage,* a charming 19th-century bungalow shaded by a giant rubber tree. Fifty feet farther down, past a blind corner, are some ponds surrounded by ancient stone walls where freshly caught fish were once stored. About a third of a mile up from the ponds, just past a steep hill, is a junction. Here you can wander up and down several lovely residential streets: Point Shares, Lone Palm Drive, or Overock Hill and Overock Drive. If you make a right turn on Point Shares Road, you'll come to another cluster of roads, including Leeside Drive, Hastings Road, and Miamba Lane. To return to Hamilton, retrace your steps on Point Shares and Fairylands Roads and turn right onto Pitts Bay Road.

Paget Pleasures

Although this sliver of land is densely populated, it's well worth a visit. Named for an English lord, it was settled relatively early, and it's possible to tour many of its lovely 17th- and 18th-century homes. You can glimpse some of these homes from the ferry, which skims along the northern coast on its way to Warwick, or you can spend a pleasant afternoon strolling the famous beaches along the southern strand.

These two pleasant walks through the parish's predominantly flat terrain cover a total of 6 miles, following old tribe roads and abandoned railway tracks. Each walk can be completed in a leisurely couple of hours. Don't forget your bathing suit, for you can swim at Elbow Beach, one of the finest sandy strands on the southern shore.

A PAGET OVERVIEW

The first of our suggested walks begins at the *Botanical Gardens of Bermuda,* a rambling 36-acre park maintained by the government. Give yourself extra time to wander through the gardens, or return sometime for a picnic; the lovely displays of palms, hibiscus, and succulents are well worth a visit (also see *Natural Wonderlands* in DIVERSIONS). The gardens are open daily from sunrise to sunset; no admission charge. Also be sure to see *Camden,* the 18th-century home that is now the Premier of Bermuda's official residence. The house is open to the public on Tuesdays and Fridays from noon to 2 PM, except when there is an official function; no admission charge (see *Historic Homes and Gardens* in DIVERSIONS).

From the gardens, turn left onto Point Finger Road, walk down about a quarter of a mile, then take a right onto South Road. In another 100 yards there's a roundabout, or traffic circle, at the southern end of Trimingham Road. (Bermuda's roundabouts are a landscape architect's dream; at their centers, colorful annuals—petunias, begonias, and colorful green and purple kale—are beautifully arranged. The plantings in the roundabouts can be changed frequently—a mixed blessing that can confuse cyclists who mark their location by the color of the blooms. Better to choose more permanent mileposts, for last Monday's "yellow" roundabout may be decked out in pink today.)

Go straight past the roundabout and climb up a slight incline bordered by oleanders and pampas grass, past Inglewood Lane. This will lead to a peaceful area where bird calls echo through the cedar, spice, and palmetto trees. The turnoff to the railway trail is just a little farther on to your right. Once on the trail, a tunnel runs under South Road and leads to a sunny path where blue and purple morning glories and hibiscus flowers cover the surrounding hills. In a quarter of a mile or so you'll cross Grape Bay Drive;

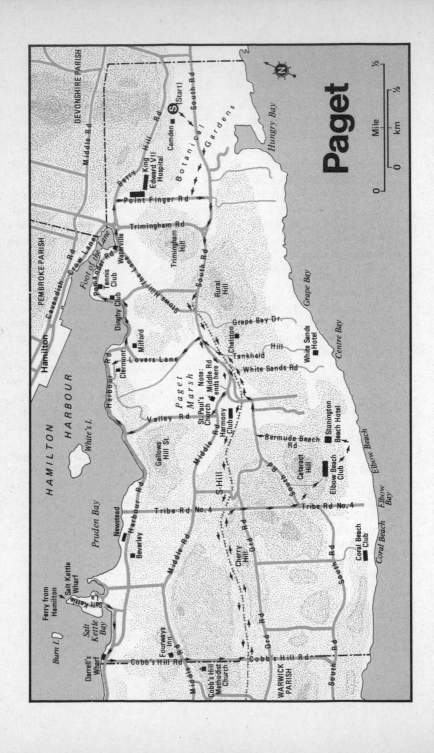

Paget

look down the drive to your left to see the gatehouse of *Chelston,* the home of the American consul general. Acquired by the US government in 1964, the 14½-acre property stretches to the South Shore. The main house and cottage, a guesthouse, a large bathhouse, stables, and a beach house occupy the grounds, which are closed to the public.

If you're in the mood for some fresh fruit, turn off to the right, head down White Sands Road for several hundred yards, and take a sharp left into the *Rural Hill Plaza Shopping Centre* on Middle Road. There is a stand there that's stocked with pawpaws, watermelons, bananas, and many other varieties of produce.

Back on the trail, walk by the hedges of hibiscus and groves of Pride of India trees and the 18th-century whitewashed cottage called *Ashley House;* soon you'll see the pretty gray steeple of *St. Paul's Church* (locals claim the church, also known as *Paget Church,* has a resident ghost). The empty tract of land to the right of *St. Paul's Church* is *Paget Marsh,* an 18-acre nature reserve. An oasis of green surrounded by buildings and roads, the reserve is home to the oldest palmetto trees on the island, as well as many species of rare plants and native and migratory birds. To arrange a tour, contact the *Bermuda National Trust* (phone: 236-6483); the ecology of the marsh is too fragile to sustain large numbers of unannounced visitors. Note the terraced whitewashed roofs of the cottages, which are designed to catch precious rainwater.

In another quarter of a mile you'll cross South Road just past the old pink railway station. Be sure to take a look at the beautifully kept beds of gladiolus, snapdragons, and petunias at *Harmony Club,* the inn on the right. Follow the trail for half a mile up to S Hill (named for the road that snakes up its slope) and continue for three-quarters of a mile to Cobb's Hill Road. The countryside here has changed little over the years; there are small vegetable plots, patches of banana trees, and an occasional rider on horseback.

The best way to reach the South Road is to retrace your steps on the railway trail toward S Hill; about 150 feet from the bottom of the hill there is a turnoff on the right to Tribe Road No. 4. Take this and climb a steep 100 yards to the intersection with Southcote Road at the top of the hill. Take a breather at the limestone moongate near the top of the Tribe Road before crossing Southcote Road, another steep stretch that lasts for several hundred yards. This was the toughest part of this walk; from here it's all downhill, with the ocean before you. Walk a few hundred yards past a banana patch to South Road. Across the road is a small park, where you can rest on a stone bench and smell the jasmine flowers. Walk down South Road for about 200 yards until the road veers sharply to the right; just at this point a road branches off straight in front of you. Take it for about a quarter of a mile until you reach the pink-and-white sands of Elbow Beach.

If you've had enough walking at this point, you can call a cab from the booth by the road to fetch you. Otherwise, take a swim or explore the half-mile stretch of beach, particularly the coral and limestone formations at the western end, where you can sit on the steps carved into the cliff. The view from there is of the cottages and clubhouse of the *Coral Beach Club,* one of the best places to play tennis on the island. The beach club is private, but courts are available for rent (see *Choice Courts* in THE ISLAND).

On the east end of the beach are two places that serve a delicious lunch: *Café Lido,* at the *Elbow Beach* hotel (phone: 236-3535), and the *Stonington Beach* hotel (phone: 236-5416), with its casual outdoor terrace and more formal *Norwood Room.* Both serve lunch from noon to 2 PM. *Stonington* is part of *Bermuda College*'s Department of Hotel Technology, and you'll be served with cheery efficiency by its students. About 50 yards from the main entrance of *Stonington* is *Art House* (phone: 236-6746), worth visiting for its prints, paintings, and lithographs of Bermuda scenes.

If you're in the mood to shop, continue down from *Stonington* onto Bermuda Beach Road for a third of a mile, take a right onto South Road, and stop in at the Paget outlet of *Trimingham's* just on the corner (phone: 236-7712). They've got a good selection of British Portmeirion china and every imaginable shade of Bermuda shorts. The prices are lower than they would be stateside, and the store will deliver (free) your purchases to your hotel. Next door is the *Bermuda Railway Company* (phone: 236-3356), which sells stylish cotton sportswear at reasonable prices. If you haven't eaten already, the *Paraquet* restaurant serves excellent fish cakes (see *Eating Out* in THE ISLAND).

Continue a few hundred yards farther down South Road to the *Modern Mart Grocery* and a bus shelter on the right. In another 20 yards or so, the railway trail will be on the right. Follow the railway path for about a quarter of a mile, then turn left onto White Sands Road. After another quarter of a mile, turn right onto South Road and walk up the hill a few hundred yards to Lovers Lane—one of the most romantic places on the island for strolling. At this point you have a choice: You can turn left onto the lane or continue for a short distance along South Road, and then take a left onto Stowe Hill Road.

If you choose to follow Lovers Lane, walk about half a mile between the narrow stone walls covered with cascading philodendrons. On the right, just before the road narrows to become one way, is *Milford,* a beautifully kept private Georgian home built by sea captain Francis John Jones IX in 1810; his direct descendants still live here. Watch the traffic as you walk down to Harbour Road. Take a right, proceed past the boatyard, and take a left onto Pomander Road. There are boats moored in Hamilton Harbour and lovely homes nestled along the shoreline.

On the half-mile stretch of Pomander Road, you'll pass the *Royal Hamilton Amateur Dinghy Club* (founded in 1882). Now a sailing club, the *Dinghy Club* originally existed solely to train crews to sail the 14-foot-long boats in competition every year. Also on Pomander Road are the private *Pomander Gate Tennis Club* and *Waterville,* an 18th-century Georgian home that is the headquarters of the *Bermuda National Trust.* Souvenirs are sold in its gift shop, which is closed Sundays and Mondays (phone: 236-6483). Rare varieties of roses grow in the garden, and ducks swim along the waterfront (bring along some bread so you can feed them).

If you choose to follow the Stowe Hill route, stop to see *Rosecote,* the home and studio of artist Alfred Birdsey, which is on the left just before the road bends to the right. You can watch him paint his Impressionist-style watercolors in his studio during the week. From Birdsey's house it's only a few hundred yards to Harbour Road, where you take a right onto Pomander Road, thus meeting up with the main route.

Continue on Pomander Road for about half a mile until it dead-ends. Walk east about 200 yards to a roundabout, where you take a left onto Foot of the Lane Road. On the left is a park overlooking the bay. Stop in for cream puffs and coconut cakes at the *Crow Lane Bakery* (phone: 292-2220), in the pink building across the street from the park, but be careful crossing the busy roadway that leads to Hamilton. To get back to your starting point, walk up The Lane for several hundred yards and turn right onto Point Finger Road. The gate to the *Botanical Gardens* is about a quarter of a mile down on the left, just past the hospital.

WESTERN PAGET

Take the ferry from Hamilton to the Salt Kettle stop to begin our second suggested walk, which traverses the western side of the parish and leads to Elbow Beach and the *Botanical Gardens.* (In the 17th century, the Salt Kettle cove was a mooring spot for vessels carrying salt from the Turks Islands. At one time, a large kettle filled with seawater stood near the ferry stop; when the seawater evaporated, salt crystals were left behind.) When you get off the ferry, turn left and walk down Salt Kettle Road, which overlooks picturesque Prudden Bay and Hamilton Harbour. Winslow Homer captured the view from here in a watercolor he painted in 1899.

Continue skirting the bay for a few hundred yards and take a right onto Salt Kettle Lane, which is lined with several historic homes. *Marechaux Cottage* is covered with limewash, which Bermudians apply to seal the walls of their homes before decorating them with pastel paints. To the left is *Salt Winds,* an 18th-century home whose verandah overlooks the road; its ground-floor rooms were hewn out of rock at water level so that ships could draw right up to the wharf to discharge their cargoes. Next door, heading west, is *The Chimneys,* with its six stone stacks; in its cellar are niches hewn out of solid rock where slaves once slept.

From Salt Kettle Lane you can watch cruise ships sail into Hamilton Harbour through the narrow channel known as Two Rock Passage, about a mile to the west of the small chain of islands. Look for the ships on Mondays between 8:30 and 10 AM from April through October.

At the end of this tranquil stretch, cross Harbour Road and turn left onto Cobb's Hill Road. Climb the hill past *Pretty Penny* inn, one of the island's nicest places to stay. On your left is *Belair,* a *National Trust* property with double verandahs and a flat roof, which is rare in Bermuda (it's not open to the public). After climbing a quarter of a mile, cross Middle Road; *Fourways,* one of Bermuda's best restaurants, is on the corner. Try the chateaubriand and sample any of their soups—they're wonderful (also see *Eating Out* in THE ISLAND). Stroll up Cobb's Hill for a few hundred yards to the *Cobb's Hill Methodist Church* on the right. Known as the "moonlight church," it was built during the early 19th century by slaves working at night when their daytime chores were done.

The hill crests just past the church, and you'll turn left onto the old railway trail about 100 yards farther on the left. Here you get a sense of what Bermuda looked like before cars were first permitted to drive on the island in 1946. You'll wander past farms growing broccoli, onions, and potatoes, for about three-quarters of a mile, and then take a right onto Tribe Road No. 4. There you pick up the trail described in the first walk.

ON TWO WHEELS

If you prefer, cycle the routes just outlined and complete them in about half the time. There are some one-way streets, though, so you'll have to deviate a little from the walking tours. At Elbow Beach, lock up your bike in the parking lot and jog on the sand or swim.

When you get to Lovers Lane, walk your bicycle down the narrow one-way stretch onto Harbour Road or skip this route entirely and pedal up South Road to Stowe Hill. Pomander Road is one way going east, so you'll have to walk your bike or turn right onto The Lane, take a left onto Pomander Road, and loop around until it meets Harbour Road.

You also can travel most of the routes just described by moped, with the exception of the railway trails, where motorized vehicles are not allowed. Here's one alternative route: From the *Botanical Gardens,* take South Road for 2 miles past Tribe Road No. 4 at Elbow Beach. Continue on South Road past the *Coral Beach Club* and turn right onto Cobb's Hill Road. Cross Ord and Middle Roads and continue for half a mile to Harbour Road. Take a right onto Harbour Road, go a quarter of a mile, then take a left onto Salt Kettle Road. Head down the hill another quarter of a mile and round the bend. You can ride down until the road dead-ends by the Salt Kettle ferry stop. Turn around and go back up Salt Kettle Road until you reach Harbour Road; take a left and follow the road back for 2 miles to the roundabout at the southeastern edge of Hamilton. You'll pass some beautiful homes along this stretch, including *Beverley,* an 18th-century Georgian home, which you'll see just before the *Newstead* hotel, one of the island's best small hostelries. There are no shoulders on the road, so if you want to take a picture, watch out for the traffic.

A few hundred yards past Lower Ferry is clay-colored *Clermont,* a 19th-century Georgian home where the first game of tennis was played on the island (and in all of North America) in 1873. When you reach the round-about, cross it and continue east up Berry Hill Road. Half a mile farther on the right is the north entrance to the *Botanical Gardens.*

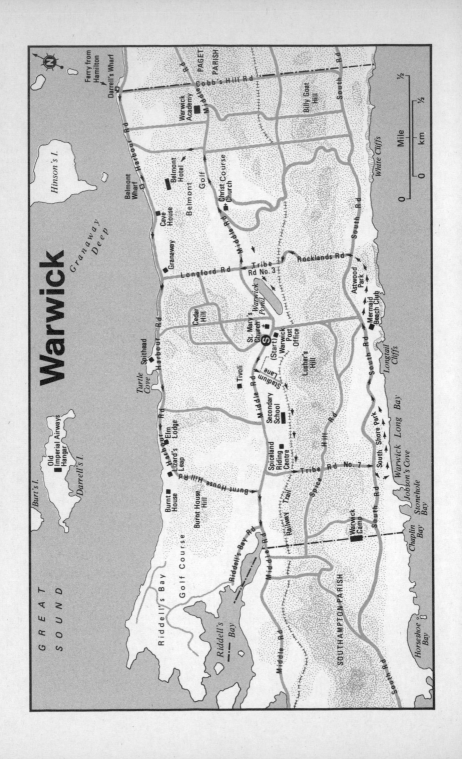

Wandering Warwick

Warwick Parish—named for Robert Rich, second Earl of Warwick—is home to some lovely out-of-the-way spots that even some Bermuda natives have never seen. Scots will feel at home here, for Warwick's two fine golf courses bear a strong resemblance to links back home, and the parish is home to the oldest Presbyterian church in British territories overseas. The parish's southern strand is bordered by the longest unbroken stretch of beach in Bermuda. We offer two walking routes through the parish.

FOREST, WETLANDS, AND SOUTHERN BEACHES

The 5-mile route described here runs through an allspice forest, a nature reserve containing one of the island's few natural saltwater ponds, and along some beautiful beaches. If your pace is brisk, you can complete the circuit in a couple of hours, or you can just as easily stop for lunch or a swim and make a day of it. If you plan to swim at Astwood Cove, Stonehole Bay, or Jobson's Cove, wear your swimsuit underneath your clothes, as there is no place to change. For the latter two beaches, however, facilities are available just over a quarter of a mile away on the western edge of Warwick Long Bay. Chaplin Bay has restroom facilities.

Start at the Warwick Post Office; take a left out of the parking lot and head down Middle Road for a quarter of a mile to Stadium Lane. There's a tempting fruit and vegetable stand there; it's closed Sundays and holidays. Across Middle Road, through a gap in the cherry trees, is *Tivoli,* an 18th-century farm—and now a school—surrounded by pastures, a marsh, and thickly wooded hillsides. (Owned by the *Bermuda National Trust,* it should be admired from the road for the sake of the tenant's privacy.)

Head south along Stadium Lane for a quarter of a mile and take the second right onto the railway trail; it's clearly marked. On the right are the grounds of the *Warwick Secondary School,* where you may spy a group of boys in gray and navy uniforms playing soccer (the path is so close to the school building that you can even see students sitting in their classrooms). To the left is *Warwick Ridge Park.* The trail then plunges into a dense grove of allspice trees (you can smell their pungent scent by crushing one of the waxy green leaves). The trees, which reach 60 feet in height, bear small clusters of berries that are dried and crushed to flavor cakes and pies.

A few hundred yards farther on is the *Spicelands Riding Centre* (phone: 238-8246). Make a mental note; you might want to return sometime for an early morning ride.

Continue west for another quarter mile and then take a left onto Tribe Road No. 7, which leads to the pristine beaches on the island's southern coast. Look for the low concrete post that marks the start of the road.

Scramble up a steep, rocky stretch for a quarter of a mile or so as the road climbs through an allspice and palmetto forest. Vegetable gardens can be seen now and then. Just as you're getting weary, the road levels off and slopes gently down and crosses Spice Hill Road. Continue south toward the ocean.

Here more spice trees shade the route; look for the abandoned buttery on the left, just before the road changes from tar to sand. These house-like structures, with their steep, stepped roofs, had thick walls to protect foodstuffs from spoiling. Watch for them; there are many still standing throughout the island, though they're no longer in use. Then climb a short hill; from the top you can see open pasture and the vast blue of the ocean beyond. From there it's an easy half mile to *South Shore Park* and one of the island's best beaches. Here, coral and limestone rocks jut out of the sea just off Warwick Long Bay. You also can explore the string of small coves just to the west of the main beach; Jobson's Cove, Stonehole Bay (named for the hole in the rock formation that is a backdrop to the beach), and Chaplin Bay are among the finest small beaches on the island. The water is calm here, and a gentle breeze blows from the south. Make another note: This stretch of beach deserves a full day for swimming, sunning, and strolling.

Walk through the parking lot behind these coves, climb the hill for 200 yards, and pick up South Road going east—the beaches will be to the right. There's a phone booth here from which you can call a cab if you like, or you can stroll along for about a quarter mile along the grass verges to the eastern end of Warwick Long Bay, enjoying the spectacular views all the way. If you're here in the spring or summer, you'll see a fuchsia-colored truck almost opposite the western entrance to the bay where you can buy snacks from midmorning to late afternoon. If you prefer more substantial fare, fish platters, salad, hamburgers, and sandwiches are served at the *Jolly Lobster* (phone: 236-1931) at the *Mermaid Beach Club,* less than half a mile to the east. It's open mid-March to mid-November from noon to 2:30 PM.

From the park above the eastern edge of the bay, walk along the South Road for a half mile or so (watch the traffic as you go). You'll pass Mermaid Beach and Longtail Cliffs on the right. Slip through the gap in the fence and shrubbery just as the road swings left and climbs uphill. This is the entrance to *Astwood Park* and the beach below, which is one of Bermuda's best. You're free to roam through the valley; it's all public land except for a solitary vegetable farm. Explore the hillsides covered with Spanish bayonets and Australian pines and make your way down to the secluded coves, taking care not to slip on the rocks. There's a phone booth in the parking lot if you're ready to call a cab.

If you're still game, continue east about a quarter of a mile along the paved park road. When you see South Road, take a right; after 50 yards turn left onto Rocklands Road. The climb is steep here, but you'll have time to admire the charming pastel cottages and bungalows along the way, and from the crest of the hill there's a broad view of the Atlantic. Continue to follow the road as it winds half a mile down to a verdant valley dotted with charming homes. Bear left onto the Bermuda Railway Trail and, after 60 feet or so, take a right onto Tribe Road No. 3. The road climbs for a few hundred yards and then dips steeply down a hill overlooking Warwick Pond. Palmetto, cedar, and allspice trees shade the path, and it's not unusual to hear a cardinal or a kiskadee.

Owned by the *Bermuda National Trust,* Warwick Pond is part of a long chain of wetlands that originally stretched from Barnes Corner in Southampton to Spittal Pond in Smith's. Fed by a subterranean channel that brings water from the sea, this area has a large population of wild birds. If you're patient, you may see an egret or a blue heron. You also can follow the dead-end path that skirts the southern edge of the pond; don't get your feet wet!

Follow the path back to Tribe Road No. 3, which soon joins up with Middle Road. Take a right and you will see the *Belmont* hotel's golf course on the left. Half a mile farther on the right is *Christ Church.* Built in 1719, it's the oldest Presbyterian church in the British overseas territories. It was here, in 1748, that a preacher named George Whitefield defied the orders of Bermuda Governor William Popple and railed against the plight of slaves. Discharged by the governor, he wrote in his farewell sermon: "What a sweet, unaffected weeping was there to be seen everywhere. . . . I believe that there were few dry eyes. The Negroes likewise . . . wept plentifully. . . . Surely a great work is begun in Bermuda. Carry it on O Lord." The pulpit from which Whitefield delivered his sermons still exists. Wander through the graveyard for a lesson in Bermuda's past. A little farther down is *Warwick Academy,* Bermuda's oldest school (ca. 1663). Among its illustrious alumni was Francis Patton, who was President of *Princeton University* from 1888 to 1913.

A quarter of a mile up on the left is the *Belmont* hotel (phone: 236-1301), where you can sip a rum swizzle before calling a cab to take you home. Or you might want to walk down the hill from the hotel to the dock, to catch the ferry to Hamilton, enjoying the harbor views and the rocky Warwick and Paget shorelines along the way.

THE NORTH SHORE

If you prefer a shorter walk, take the following route, which covers between 3 and 5 miles, depending on whether you go to Riddell's Bay Peninsula on Warwick's north shore. It's best to set out between 10 AM and 3 PM, when traffic is light, since there are few sidewalks. This scenic route leads past the former homes of playwrights Eugene O'Neill and Noël Coward and by Bermuda's original airport, which was closed in 1941.

Start at *Darrell's Wharf,* which is reachable by ferry from Hamilton. The work of local artists is on display at *Jaqui's Art Studio* (phone: 234-4068), just to the left from the whitewashed shelter on the dock. Note the Georgian architecture of *Blackburn Place,* an 18th-century home across the street.

Its two front wings were added in 1820 by Nathaniel Darrell, a sea captain who moored his ship at *Darrell's Wharf.* The upper floor of the house was used as living quarters and the ground floor served as a warehouse and offices. Darrell is believed to have planted the bay grape in front of the house. Make a right onto Harbour Road, crossing the sidewalk at the blind corner about 200 yards up the road. After you pass *Kempdon,* the yellow home on the right, look across Granaway Deep to Hinson's Island (several private islands dot the bay). To the west, closer to the shoreline, is Darrell's Island, site of Bermuda's first airport, where seaplanes run by *Pan American* and *Imperial Airways* first landed in 1938. Named "Dorrel" on Richard Norwood's first survey map (for John Dorrel, who owned properties in Pembroke, Paget, Southampton, and Warwick parishes), Darrell's Island was the site of an internment camp for more than 1,000 South African Boer prisoners during the Boer War. Many of them were talented woodcarvers; their work is on display at the *Bermuda Historical Society Museum* in the city of Hamilton (see *Historical Homes and Gardens* in DIVERSIONS). The museum is closed Sundays; no admission charge (phone: 295-2487).

From this point you can still see the old airline terminal building at the water's edge, and the boat slip at its eastern end, which was used for seaplanes. Also within view are Hawkins's, Burt's, and Marshall's Islands, once owned by the Royal Navy; Marshall's is now privately owned by a British family.

Several hundred yards down the hill is a boatyard where you're likely to see a sailboat being repaired. A short distance on is the *Belmont Wharf* ferry stop. Slate-roofed cottages line the road; *Cave House,* on the left about 400 yards past the ferry, is named for a grotto discovered on the property. As with *Blackburn Place,* the upstairs rooms were used as living quarters; the ground-level warehouse stored cargo brought by ships into nearby Granaway Deep. The water in this harbor is so clear that you may see a snapper or two.

At the intersection with Longford Road, about a quarter of a mile farther on, is *Granaway,* an 18th-century home built by Capt. Hezekiah Frith for his daughter, Mehitabel. A "welcoming arms" staircase leads to the main entrance. Far out on a point half a mile farther on stands *Spithead,* a pale pink, late-18th–century Bermuda homestead built by Frith, who also owned the land that now belongs to the *Belmont* golf course. *Spithead* was the winter home of Eugene O'Neill and his family during the 1920s. O'Neill's daughter, Oona (widow of comedian Charlie Chaplin), was born here. Noël Coward, who moved to Bermuda in 1956, also lived here and at *Spithead Lodge* next door.

All along this stretch palmettos wave in the breeze, and Mexican pepper trees arch over the path. There are several lovely gardens; hibiscus and honeysuckle flowers flourish in old quarries across from *Turtle Cove* and *Fleetwood Manor.*

Continue along Harbour Road past Tamarind Vale. You'll pass *Elm Lodge,* another fine example of 18th-century Bermudian architecture, on the left just before you reach Burnt House Hill. Continue on Harbour Road past *Chameleon Corners* and *Lizard's Leap* until you reach Burnt House Drive, a quiet road with a white house at the end. Natives say the original house was destroyed in 1616 by a fire lit to exterminate vermin. The steep 400-yard climb to the top of Burnt House Hill is worth the time, for it yields an impressive view of the Great Sound.

The remaining half-mile stretch of Burnt House Hill is all downhill. At the bottom, take a right and cross Middle Road to *White & Sons* grocery store (phone: 238-1050), a good place to buy a cool drink and snacks. You can call a cab from there or hop on a bus; you'll see stops on both sides of the street.

If you've still got sufficient time and energy, walk a quarter of a mile down Middle Road to Riddell's Bay Road. This stretch is lined with lovely homes; soon you'll see the emerald lawns of *Riddell's Bay* golf course on the right (see *Top Tee-Off Spots* in THE ISLAND).

ON TWO WHEELS

It's not easy to cycle along our first walking route because stretches of Tribe Road No. 7 are infuriatingly steep, and it's cumbersome to have to push a bike over the rocky trail. Cyclists and moped riders can follow part of the second route by starting at Warwick Camp. Cycle 3 miles east on South Road to the quiet residential lane called Cobb's Hill Road. Take a left and continue a mile and a half until you reach Harbour Road. You'll encounter only two hills on this stretch: the first just past the South Road junction and the second a few hundred yards beyond the intersection with Ord Road. At Harbour Road, take a left and pick up the second part of the walking route.

You can also make a detour to Warwick Pond. Take a left onto Middle Road from Burnt House Hill and ride just under 2 miles to Longford Road. Turn right, and you'll see the pond several hundred yards up on the right.

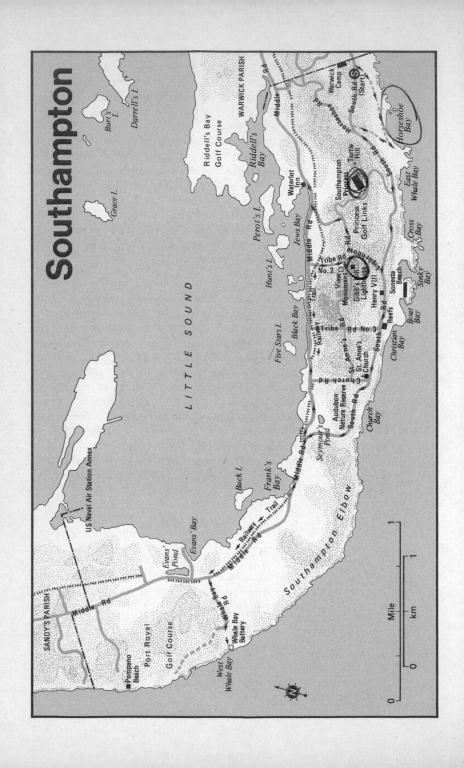

Southampton

LITTLE SOUND

Burt's I.

Darrell's I.

Grace I.

Riddell's Bay Golf Course

WARWICK PARISH

Middle Rd

Warwick Camp

South Rd

S (Start)

Horseshoe Bay

Riddell's Bay

Perot's I.

Jews Bay

Waterlot Inn

Southampton Princess

Turtle Hill

East Whale Bay

Hunt's I.

Middle Rd

Princess Golf Links

Cross Bay

Black Bay

Five Stars I.

Trail

Tribe Rd No. 2

View Rd

Monument

Railway Trail

Gibb's Hill Lighthouse

Henry VIII

Sonesta Beach

Sinky Bay

Boat Bay

Tribe Rd No. 3

St. Anne's Rd

St. Anne's Church

South Rd

Reefs

Christian Bay

Church Rd

Church Bay

Audubon Nature Reserve

South Rd

Seymour's Pond

Buck I.

Middle Rd

Evans Bay

Frank's Bay

Railway Trail

Middle Rd

Southampton Elbow

US Naval Air Station Annex

Evans Pond

SANDY'S PARISH

Middle Rd

Pompano Beach

Port Royal Golf Course

Whale Bay Rd

Whale Bay Battery

West Whale Bay

N

0   Mile   1

0   km   1

Savoring Southampton

This windswept parish in western Bermuda is named for Henry Wriothesley (pronounced *Rox*-lee), the Third Earl of Southampton, a member of the Virginia Company who brought many settlers to the island during the 17th century. In the early days, the parish was known as Port Royal. Bordered by some of the colony's finest beaches, it is also renowned for its rich soil, which attracted many farmers to the area. When surveyor Richard Norwood drew the colony's parish lines in 1616, a slice of land near the Southampton border in neighboring Sandys Parish was deemed "overplus" and was seized by Governor Daniel Tucker. When shareholders of the Bermuda Company protested, Tucker reluctantly parted with most of the land. (The Tucker family seems to have had an opportunistic streak. During the American Revolution, Colonel Henry Tucker, a descendant of the governor, stole gunpowder from the British and shipped it to George Washington.) The land on which the US Naval Air Station Annex is located was once known as Tucker's Island. The first of our routes covers the eastern portion of the parish; the second, shorter, route covers the west.

EASTERN SOUTHAMPTON

This walking tour through Southampton covers about 7½ miles, leading past the spectacular beaches at Horseshoe and Church Bays, the *Gibb's Hill Lighthouse,* and an *Audubon Society* nature reserve. You can ride a bike or moped along most of this route, but mopeds aren't allowed on the tribe road to the lighthouse or the railway trail.

The walk begins on South Road near *Warwick Camp,* the headquarters of the Bermuda Regiment. Across from the camp's sentry box is a road that leads to a sandy trail that meanders past the rocks to Horseshoe Bay Beach. Go for a swim along this perfectly curved strand, said to be one of the most photographed in the world; the surf isn't unpleasantly rough, and the water is shallow close to shore. Don't dive from the rocky outcroppings, though; there's often a dangerous surge around them. Just offshore lies a 6-mile area of reef known locally as "boilers," where the surf melts into a seething mass of foam. If you should be here over the *Easter* holidays, don't miss the kite festival that takes place here on *Good Friday* (for details, see *Quintessential Bermuda* in DIVERSIONS).

Walk barefoot down the fine pink sand to the west end of the beach, where there's a small restaurant, changing rooms, and a souvenir shop. From here there's a spectacular view of Southampton and the Warwick coast. If you'd like to play tennis, try the courts just to the northeast (phone: 238-0572). Scuba divers can rent equipment and hire a guide here.

To continue the walk, follow Horseshoe Road, which is bordered by

Spanish bayonets and oleanders, up the hill for half a mile to South Road. Stay to the left to take advantage of the fine views of the coast. After a mile or so the road bends sharply to the right, and you'll see the *Southampton Princess* hotel and its 18-hole executive golf course. From there it's half a mile to *Henry VIII,* a lively English pub where several varieties of ale are on tap; try the roast beef and Yorkshire pudding or the steak Anne Boleyn (see *Eating Out* in THE ISLAND). A little farther on is the *Sonesta Beach* hotel; the sheltered cove near the western end is a good place to practice scuba diving. Nearby is *Reefs,* one of Bermuda's favorite hotels, where you can sit under a thatch palm roof at *Coconuts,* a fine seafood restaurant, and watch the waves crash on the beach (also see *Eating Out* in THE ISLAND).

Continuing westward on South Road, you'll spy many luxurious cliffside homes; note the terracing on the roofs, which is designed to direct precious rainwater to underground cisterns. Half a mile farther on stands *St. Anne's Church.* Built in 1616, it's one of the oldest Anglican churches in the colony. Take a rubbing or two of its weathered slate gravestones. Just beyond *St. Anne's,* across Church Road, there's a park with a wonderful view of the coast. In the summer and early fall, you can sit in the shade of the Australian pines and watch longtails–native birds with sweeping black-and-white tail feathers—diving from the nearby cliffs. (If you like you can take a shortcut here: Take Church Road north directly to Middle Road; this shaves a mile and a quarter off this route.)

Walk through the park and climb down a steep hill for a few hundred yards to the beach, which is one of the best on the island. The coarse sand is flecked with pink, and it's a good place to body-surf, but watch the strong undertow. The reefs just offshore shelter dozens of varieties of fish; bring your snorkeling and diving gear. Continue walking along South Road; after about half a mile it turns sharply to the north and joins Middle Road. (Look for the fisherman who often sells fresh grouper, snapper, and rockfish on the corner on Thursdays and Fridays.)

Here you can look out to the north over the rocky coast along Little Sound. Head east on Middle Road; about a half mile down on the right is the entrance to *Seymour's Pond Nature Reserve,* a 2½-acre parcel owned by the *Bermuda Audubon Society.* If you're patient, you might spy an egret or an eastern bluebird. Weatherbeaten cedars and pepper trees line the road just past the pond. Cross Church Road (where folks who took the shortcut rejoin the main route) and you'll see an entrance to the railway trail, where you can forage for wild fennel. Farther along to the left you'll catch glimpses of the coast and of Five Star Island (if you look carefully you can make out a white house with yellow shutters perched on this little isle). Black Bay, where some old shipwrecks lie, is half a mile farther on. Ignore the fork that descends to Black Bay; take the path that leads straight ahead until you come to a break in the trees. From here you can look down on Jew's Bay, where many yachts and fishing boats bob in the harbor.

Take a right at the crossroads, then follow the sign to *Gibb's Hill*

Lighthouse. This route runs on Tribe Road No. 2, a steep road shaded by fiddlewoods and palmettos that peters out into a narrow path that leads to a flight of stone steps. At the top of this hill there's a plaque marking "The Queen's View." On this spot, in November 1953, Queen Elizabeth II stopped to admire the vista of the sound, which is magnificent indeed. From this vantage point, you can see *Riddell's Bay* golf course and Perot's Island, which was once owned by the father of William Bennett Perot, Bermuda's first postmaster general.

For an even finer view, climb the 185 steps up the circular staircase of the lighthouse (not for the faint of heart). The 117-foot tower, which stands 245 feet above sea level, is made of cast-iron plates manufactured in London; it has been in continuous operation since May 1, 1846. In the early years, it sent out a feeble beacon generated by a kerosene lamp; the first electric light was installed in 1952. Today, a 1,500-watt bulb casts a beam that can be seen 40 miles out to sea; the light revolves 360 degrees every 50 seconds. The keeper and his assistant can explain the mechanism of the light, which is amplified by a series of prisms. The building adjacent to the lighthouse was once a signal station operated by the British Army. The lighthouse is closed holidays; no admission charge for children under 5. The *Lighthouse Tea Room* (phone: 238-8679), located in the former lighthouse keeper's cottage, serves breakfast, lunch, and afternoon tea; it is also closed holidays.

From the lighthouse, walk northeast on Lighthouse Road just under a mile to the intersection with Middle Road and the *Waterlot,* a restaurant in a restored 17th-century home where Mark Twain and Eleanor Roosevelt once dined (not together!). Walk its gardens, which are fragrant with sweet peas and gladiolus, or stop in for lunch or Sunday brunch (see *Eating Out* in THE ISLAND and *Quintessential Bermuda* in DIVERSIONS). The restaurant is usually closed January through April. Across the street stands an 18th-century dwelling called *Angel Steps.* Near this junction you can catch a bus or hail a cab.

WESTERN SOUTHAMPTON

The western reaches of Southampton are also worth exploring. This 4-mile route begins at the *Seymour's Pond Nature Reserve.* Walk west on Middle Road past the reserve and the South Road intersection; proceed about half a mile past Frank's Bay to see the remains of an old railway trestle. Turn right onto the railway trail and walk for just over a mile past carefully tended vegetable gardens and stands of palmetto and Australian pine. You'll see *Buckingham,* a 17th-century farmhouse with a traditional "welcoming arms" entrance, on the right. Make a left onto Whale Bay Road and walk for half a mile to the bay. During the 17th and 18th centuries, whalers towed pilot and sperm whales here to be processed. The bay is small and secluded—a must for snorkelers. On the western edge of the beach stands the *Whale Bay Battery,* a derelict 19th-century garrison built by British engineers to protect the *Royal Naval Dockyard.*

Retrace your steps to Middle Road, then take a left. Walk about half a mile to the intersection with Tribe Road No. 5; it's on the right just before the gas station. Go up the incline and take a left on the railway trail, about 100 feet. Take the trail through the woods past a playing field on the left; after about three-quarters of a mile turn left at the main entrance to the US Naval Air Station Annex onto George's Bay Road; turn left again onto Middle Road. Stroll down for half a mile to Pompano Beach Road; the *Pompano Beach Club* (phone: 234-0222) is on the left in about a half a mile. The government-owned 18-hole *Port Royal* golf course, one of the island's best, is nearby (also see *Top Tee-Off Spots* in THE ISLAND). If time permits, you can explore 19th-century *Whale Bay Fort* on the edge of the greens; you can also stop at *Port Royal* for a game of tennis. From here you can call a cab or head back to Middle Road and take a bus to your hotel.

Stepping Out in Sandys

Sandys—it's pronounced as if there were no y—is commonly called Somerset Parish. It's composed of four islands: Somerset, the largest and southernmost, which is named for Admiral Sir George Somers, who was shipwrecked on Bermuda in 1609; Watford; Boaz; and Ireland Island, site of the *Royal Naval Dockyard* (which locals refer to as simply the *Dockyard*). The parish was named for Sir Edwin Sandys, a shareholder of the Bermuda Company who persuaded many English families to immigrate to Bermuda in the early 17th century.

The independent-minded residents of Sandys have long had a contrary streak. During the American Civil War, for instance, most Bermudians sided with Jefferson Davis, but the residents of Sandys staunchly supported the Union cause.

The scenery here is some of the most beautiful in Bermuda, and there are historic forts, a quaint town, and secluded coves to explore. The three routes described here can be covered on foot or by bicycle or moped. The first runs the length of Somerset Island, the second focuses on the *Dockyard,* and the third covers the trip from the *Dockyard* back to Somerset.

SOMERSET ISLAND

To begin our first tour, take the ferry from Hamilton to Somerset Bridge; it is the first stop in Sandys Parish. Before beginning the walk, turn south to cross the drawbridge, which, though it is just wide enough to let sailboats through, is never used (see *Quintessential Bermuda* in DIVERSIONS). Take a look at the old Somerset Post Office, an 18th-century cottage called *Crossways,* and the Georgian-style *Bridge House,* now the Anglican rectory; then recross the bridge and walk up Somerset Road for 70 yards or so to the railway trail, which branches off to the right.

This stretch of the railway trail leads through some of the loveliest scenery on the island. As you start off, you'll walk through fragrant groves of allspice and Australian pine, past several pastel-colored homes. About a quarter of a mile down on the right is the *Lantana Colony Club,* one of the most exclusive cottage colonies in Bermuda. You can lunch here on the terrace, or dine in the glass-roofed conservatory lit by Venetian glass lamps that are shaped like grape clusters (see *Eating Out* in THE ISLAND).

Two hundred yards farther on is a trail to the left that leads to *Fort Scaur.* Take this trail (if you have a bike or moped, stash it at the foot of the trail) and climb about 150 yards up a thickly wooded slope, past a boundary stone set down in 1906. The fort sits atop the highest hill in Somerset (for details, see *Touring Bermuda's Forts* in DIVERSIONS). If you like, follow the trail east across the railway trail to the rocky shore of the Great Sound, where you can take a dip in the ocean or try to catch a snapper or two.

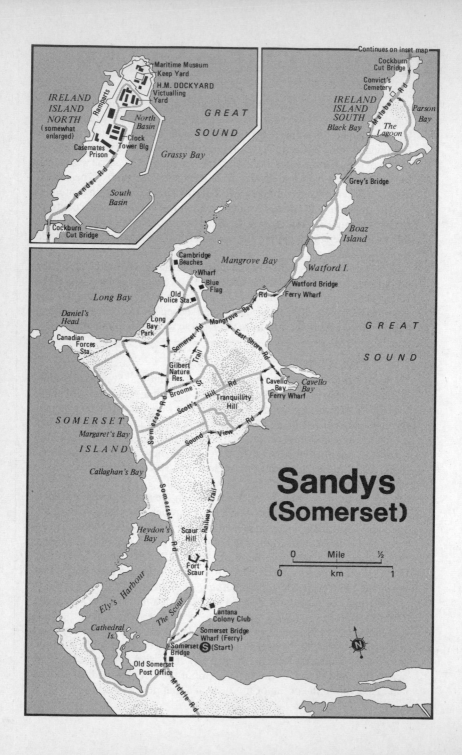

**Sandys
(Somerset)**

Maritime Museum
Keep Yard
H.M. DOCKYARD
Victualling
Yard

*IRELAND
ISLAND
NORTH*
(somewhat
enlarged)

Ramparts

North
Basin

Casemates
Prison

Clock
Tower Blg

Pender Rd

South
Basin

Cockburn
Cut Bridge

GREAT

SOUND

Grassy Bay

Continues on inset map

Cockburn
Cut Bridge

Convict's
Cemetery

*IRELAND
ISLAND
SOUTH*

Black Bay

*The
Lagoon*

Malabar Rd

*Parson
Bay*

Grey's Bridge

*Boaz
Island*

Watford I.

Watford Bridge
Ferry Wharf

Rd

Cambridge
Beaches

Wharf

Blue
Flag

Old
Police Sta.

Long Bay

Mangrove Bay

Long
Bay
Park

Somerset Rd

Mangrove Bay Rd

East Shore Rd

GREAT

SOUND

*Daniel's
Head*

Canadian
Forces
Sta.

Trail

Gilbert
Nature
Res.

Broome St

Rd

Cavello
Bay
Ferry Wharf

*Cavello
Bay*

Scott's
Hill

Tranquillity
Hill

SOMERSET

Margaret's Bay

ISLAND

View

Sound

Rd

Callaghan's Bay

Somerset Rd

0   Mile   ½

0   km   1

*Heydon's
Bay*

Railway Trail

Scaur
Hill

Somerset Rd

Fort
Scaur

Ely's Harbour

The Scaur

Lantana
Colony Club

Somerset Bridge
Wharf (Ferry)

*Cathedral
Is.*

Somerset
Bridge

S (Start)

Old Somerset
Post Office

Middle Rd

N

Make your way back to the trail and continue northward for a mile or so through stands of cedars and allspice trees. Take a right on Sound View Road and continue up this quiet residential street lined with many fine homes. Make a wide arc past Tranquillity Hill and Gwelly and Saltsea Lanes, passing *Four Winds,* a cinnamon-colored house built in 1937, on the right; note the Italian statuary in the garden. Take a right on Scott's Hill Road and walk about 75 yards to East Shore Road. At the junction of the two, take the small road branching off to the right called Cavello Lane; it leads to Cavello Bay, a sheltered cove fringed with cedars and palmettos. The ferry stops here, and you can climb aboard and continue on to Watford Bridge and the *Dockyard.*

If you prefer to walk, return to East Shore Road and head north past *Somerwood,* a gray 17th-century home with blue shutters and a "welcoming arms" staircase. In half a mile you'll reach sleepy Somerset Village on Mangrove Bay, where there are a few restaurants and a small selection of shops. A good place to enjoy a bowl of fish chowder is on the terrace overlooking the bay at the *Loyalty Inn,* near the junction of East Shore Road and Mangrove Bay Road; or try the steak and kidney pie at the *Somerset Country Squire,* about 200 yards farther west. (For details about both places, see *Eating Out* in THE ISLAND.) If you continue walking west past Mangrove Bay Beach, which is lined with coconut palms—alas, the old mangrove trees are gone!—there's a green home with a semicircular staircase that was once the parish police station and jail. Beyond it are several fine old homes, including *Blue Flag,* a 17th-century mansion that was once a pub for naval officers.

When you reach Cambridge Road, make a right and walk down the wharf, where you can see the azure waters of the bay (the beach is private along this stretch). There's a phone on the wharf if you're ready to call a cab, or you can continue west on Cambridge Road until you reach *Cambridge Beaches,* a cottage resort with an excellent restaurant (see *Eating Out* in THE ISLAND). There's an old stone moongate to the left of the entrance; just beyond it is the *Irish Linen Shop* (phone: 234-0127). In just under half a mile, Cambridge Road meets Daniel's Head Road. From Daniel's Head Road, there are paths that lead to the right to *Somerset Long Bay Park* and the *Audubon Society Nature Reserve* (which is not marked). You can swim here in the calm shallow water (there are places to change on the beach) or continue this walk, heading south down Somerset Road. After Cambridge Road joins Somerset Road, continue on Somerset for about an eighth of a mile. Turn left on Broome Street and after a quarter of a mile take another left onto the railway trail, which meanders through the woods of the *Gilbert Nature Reserve,* where bluebirds and white-eyed vireos call from the fiddlewood trees. Turn left onto Beacon Hill Road and right on Somerset Road, which leads back to Mangrove Bay and the village of Somerset. From there you can catch a bus back to Somerset Bridge or continue north from the Watford Bridge to the *Dockyard.*

ROYAL NAVAL DOCKYARD

There is so much to see at the *Dockyard* that it's best to spend an afternoon strolling through it. The *Dockyard* is located at the northern tip of Ireland Island, which was known as "Hibernia" during the early days of the colony. Few people inhabited this remote isle until the early 19th century; those who occupied the island at that time lived in simple wooden houses with palmetto leaf thatch. In 1809, Royal Engineers broke ground for the naval installations, and for the next century and a half the island bustled with activity (for a description of the *Dockyard*'s history, see *Touring Bermuda's Forts* in DIVERSIONS). After World War II, the *Dockyard* lost its strategic value, and in 1953 the Royal Navy sold it to the Bermuda government for £750,000. Open daily; no admission charge (phone: 234-1418).

This tour begins by the bus stop just inside the entrance gate to the *Dockyard,* near Casemates Prison, Bermuda's largest correctional facility. To the north is the *Clock Tower Building,* whose Italianate twin towers are topped with onion domes. The recently restored north tower houses a large clock; the south displays a schedule of the tides. Today, the *Clock Tower* also houses a variety of shops and restaurants.

The slip and ferry stop are just north of the *Clock Tower.* On the north side of the slip is the Victualling Yard, where the navy stored staples in the event of a siege (prior to the mid-19th century, provisions were stored on floating hulks just offshore). Here you can see the brick and limestone houses where British naval officers once lived, and the cooperage, where stout barrels were made for the Navy's larders. Watch ceramics being fired at *Island Pottery* (phone: 234-3361), located on Freeport Road to the left of the Victualling Yard a few hundred yards from the slip. Just around the corner to the right is the *Bermuda Arts Centre* (phone: 234-2809). The *Craft Market* (phone: 234-3208), located next door, sells Bermudian wares. Beside the market is the *Neptune Cinema* (phone: 234-2923), which screens current American and international films.

The keep, located just across from the *Craft Market,* is perhaps the finest structure in the *Dockyard.* Tenders from war ships sailed here through a water gate into a protected lagoon, where they were loaded with munitions. Walk along the 30-foot ramparts and look down on the portcullis that protected the water gate. You also can explore the ordnance buildings surrounding the keep, most of which now house exhibitions. Behind it is the *Bermuda Maritime Museum* (see *Museums* in THE ISLAND).

Several hundred yards behind the museum, near the marina and the new dock for cruise ships, are the offices of *Dive Bermuda* (phone: 234-0225), which takes visitors on scuba diving tours of offshore wrecks, and of the 85-foot submarine *Enterprise* (phone: 234-3547), which offers 2½-hour underwater tours of the *Dockyard.* Stop in at the *Morning Light Emporium* (phone: 234-4150) to see its eclectic selection of local artwork, crafts, sweaters, and glassware; if hunger strikes, go next door to the *Let's Live Health Shoppe* and sample its natural foods and homemade frozen yogurt.

When you've had your fill of sightseeing, return to the Victualling Yard, where you can catch a ferry or bus back to Hamilton. Those who prefer walking or cycling can follow the next route.

THE DOCKYARD TO SOMERSET

The spectacular scenery along the 4-mile route from the *Dockyard* to Somerset Village reminds some visitors of the Florida Keys. You'll pass several beaches on the way, so wear a bathing suit under your clothes. Exit the south entrance to the *Dockyard* and walk down Pender Road for half a mile, crossing Cockburn's Cut Bridge to Ireland Island South. If you're walking, continue straight on Cochrane Road, which is one way; you'll pass a small cemetery where convicts who built the *Dockyard* were buried (look for the gravestone that says "Killed One Day, Died the Next"). If you're on a bike or moped, make a left onto Cockburn Road, which becomes Malabar Road, where you'll pass several yellow houses where Royal Naval officers live. The roads join up again north of *Lagoon Park,* a 3½-acre nature reserve crisscrossed with walking trails. There's a large graveyard here where men serving in the Royal Navy, including four admirals, are buried.

Near the cemetery is a small bridge over a narrow channel that leads from the lagoon to the ocean. A physician at the Royal Naval Hospital had the channel cut in the mid-19th century to reduce the "miasmas and vapors" thought to be responsible for the plague of yellow fever sweeping the parish. The doctor's plan was successful, for it cleared the lagoon of stagnant water, killing the mosquitoes that carried the disease. There are some mosquito-less beaches where you can swim at Black Bay, just north of the lagoon.

Cross Grey's Bridge onto Boaz Island, then continue down Malabar Road. To the right are the islands strung out off Mangrove Bay, and to the left stands the old Royal Naval Hospital, where thousands of yellow fever victims were treated in the 1850s; it is now a retirement home. Take a left onto Kitchener Road; from here you can look out over the broad expanse of the Great Sound. Several of the offshore islands were a quarantine area for ships sailing to Bermuda from the West Indies, where yellow fever and dysentery were once rife; other islands housed prisoners from South Africa during the Boer War. Proceed for half a mile to Runway Lane if you want to catch the ferry. Or make a left onto Malabar Road and walk 100 yards to *New Woody's Drive-In* (phone: 234-2082), a seafood place popular with the locals. Make a left onto Malabar Road, and then continue south for just under a mile until you cross Watford Bridge. There's a phone at the dock where you can call a cab, or you can catch the bus or a ferry back to Hamilton.

Index

Index